Citrix XenApp Performance Essentials

A practical guide for tuning and optimizing
the performance of XenApp farms using
real-world examples

Luca Dentella

PUBLISHING

BIRMINGHAM - MUMBAI

Citrix XenApp Performance Essentials

First published: August 2013

Production Reference: 1120813

Published by Packt Publishing Ltd.
Livery Place
35 Livery Street
Birmingham B3 2PB, UK.

ISBN 978-1-78217-044-0

www.packtpub.com

Cover Image by Abhishek Pandey (abhishek.pandey1210@gmail.com)

Credits

Author
Luca Dentella

Reviewer
Andy Paul

Acquisition Editor
Pramila Balan

Commissioning Editor
Llewellyn Rozario

Technical Editors
Sanhita Sawant
Sonali S. Vernekar

Copy Editors
Adithi Shetty
Laxmi Subramanian

Project Coordinator
Suraj Bist

Proofreader
Amy Guest

Indexer
Hemangini Bari

Graphics
Ronak Dhruv
Abhinash Sahu

Production Coordinator
Manu Joseph

Cover Work
Manu Joseph

About the Author

Luca Dentella is an IT architect working for an Italian consulting company, Sorint.lab.

He graduated in Telecommunication engineering from the Polytechnic University of Milan and he specialized in Windows and virtualization technologies, becoming both a Microsoft and a VMWare Certified Professional.

In the last five years, he worked mainly for INGDirect, Italy, where he helped to design and develop the IT infrastructure. Some projects he was involved in include call center virtualization, design of bank shops infrastructure, and outsourcing part of the back office.

He also worked as a Java/C# developer, and now he administers Java Application Servers such as IBM WebSphere and RedHat JBoss, and uses his programming skills to write scripts and programs for automating administrative tasks.

He designs, implements, and administers XenApp farms for different customers.

I'd like to thank my family and my girlfriend for supporting me during the writing of this book. Special thanks goes to my colleagues Albino, Aldo, and Marco who helped me in understanding network and security concepts and suggested the use of WANem.

About the Reviewer

Andy Paul is an accomplished virtualization architect, instructor and speaker. He has designed and delivered virtualization projects for Fortune 500 companies, public and private healthcare organizations, and institutions of higher education. He has also served as a lead technical trainer, an adjunct professor, and a guest speaker for multiple organizations.

Andy is currently the Virtualization Practice Director at GlassHouse Technologies, where he manages the delivery teams, oversees project architecture, and also is a VDI subject matter expert.

Visit Andy's Blog at www.paultechnologies.com/blog.

I would like to thank my wife, Mandy, for her support and dedication which has enabled me in all of my professional pursuits.

www.PacktPub.com

Support files, eBooks, discount offers and more

You might want to visit www.PacktPub.com for support files and downloads related to your book.

Did you know that Packt offers eBook versions of every book published, with PDF and ePub files available? You can upgrade to the eBook version at www.PacktPub.com and as a print book customer, you are entitled to a discount on the eBook copy. Get in touch with us at service@packtpub.com for more details.

At www.PacktPub.com, you can also read a collection of free technical articles, sign up for a range of free newsletters and receive exclusive discounts and offers on Packt books and eBooks.

http://PacktLib.PacktPub.com

Do you need instant solutions to your IT questions? PacktLib is Packt's online digital book library. Here, you can access, read and search across Packt's entire library of books.

Why Subscribe?

- Fully searchable across every book published by Packt
- Copy and paste, print and bookmark content
- On demand and accessible via web browser

Free Access for Packt account holders

If you have an account with Packt at www.PacktPub.com, you can use this to access PacktLib today and view nine entirely free books. Simply use your login credentials for immediate access.

Instant Updates on New Packt Books

Get notified! Find out when new books are published by following @PacktEnterprise on Twitter, or the *Packt Enterprise* Facebook page.

Table of Contents

Preface

Citrix XenApp is an application-delivery solution that allows apps to be virtualized, centralized, and managed in the datacenter.

A critical task every Citrix administrator has to perform is to design and maintain an infrastructure that performs well; poor performances have a high impact on users' satisfaction.

What this book covers

Chapter 1, Designing a Scalable XenApp Infrastructure, helps IT architects design a good XenApp infrastructure.

Chapter 2, Monitoring and Improving Server Performances, helps XenApp administrators monitor XenApp servers and fine-tune them for best performance.

Chapter 3, Optimizing Session Startup, helps XenApp administrators reduce the session start-up time.

Chapter 4, Improving End User Experience, helps XenApp administrators improve the end user experience.

Chapter 5, Optimizing for WAN Links, helps XenApp administrators optimize and test XenApp farms for WAN users.

What you need for this book

This book covers the latest version of Citrix XenApp 6.5, but some of the optimizations described are applicable for previous versions too. During the writing of this book, particular attention was given to pointing out which features are available only in XenApp 6.5 or with a particular licensing.

Who this book is for

This book is for IT architects and administrators who need a quick guide to design and optimize XenApp farms.

It helps to design and maintain a scalable, high-performing XenApp infrastructure with guidelines and tips to optimize system loads, sessions, and user experience.

A chapter is dedicated to WAN links, with specific suggestions about how to optimize and test farms in that scenario.

Conventions

In this book, you will find a number of styles of text that distinguish between different kinds of information. Here are some examples of these styles, and an explanation of their meaning.

Code words in text are shown as follows: "They consist of a `.vhd` file (contains the data of the virtual disk)."

Any command-line input or output is written as follows:

```
D:\Support\debug> QueryDS /table:LMS_ServerLoadTable
```

New terms and **important words** are shown in bold. Words that you see on the screen, in menus or dialog boxes for example, appear in the text like this: " You can change the priority of a policy from the context menu or from the **Actions** pane".

 Warnings or important notes appear in a box like this.

Tips and tricks appear like this.

Reader feedback

Feedback from our readers is always welcome. Let us know what you think about this book—what you liked or may have disliked. Reader feedback is important for us to develop titles that you really get the most out of.

To send us general feedback, simply send an e-mail to feedback@packtpub.com, and mention the book title via the subject of your message.

If there is a topic that you have expertise in and you are interested in either writing or contributing to a book, see our author guide on www.packtpub.com/authors.

Customer support

Now that you are the proud owner of a Packt book, we have a number of things to help you to get the most from your purchase.

Errata

Although we have taken every care to ensure the accuracy of our content, mistakes do happen. If you find a mistake in one of our books—maybe a mistake in the text or the code—we would be grateful if you would report this to us. By doing so, you can save other readers from frustration and help us improve subsequent versions of this book. If you find any errata, please report them by visiting http://www.packtpub. com/submit-errata, selecting your book, clicking on the **errata submission form** link, and entering the details of your errata. Once your errata are verified, your submission will be accepted and the errata will be uploaded on our website, or added to any list of existing errata, under the Errata section of that title. Any existing errata can be viewed by selecting your title from http://www.packtpub.com/support.

Piracy

Piracy of copyright material on the Internet is an ongoing problem across all media. At Packt, we take the protection of our copyright and licenses very seriously. If you come across any illegal copies of our works, in any form, on the Internet, please provide us with the location address or website name immediately so that we can pursue a remedy.

Please contact us at copyright@packtpub.com with a link to the suspected pirated material.

We appreciate your help in protecting our authors, and our ability to bring you valuable content.

Questions

You can contact us at questions@packtpub.com if you are having a problem with any aspect of the book, and we will do our best to address it.

1
Designing a Scalable XenApp Infrastructure

The design of a XenApp infrastructure is a complex task that requires a good knowledge of XenApp components. Taking the right decisions in the design phase may also greatly help system administrators to expand XenApp farms for satisfying new business requirements or to improve the user experience.

In this chapter you will learn:

- The key components of a XenApp infrastructure
- How those components work together
- The best practices by Citrix and some suggestions from my experience to design an architecture that respects initial requirements and is scalable for new needs
- How to implement Provisioning Services to deploy new session host servers
- How to run a load test using Citrix Load Testing

XenApp infrastructure

A XenApp infrastructure is composed of two main elements:

- Servers that publish applications (session hosts)
- Servers that run infrastructure services (controllers)

Regardless of your farm size, it is recommended to have at least one server dedicated to infrastructure services.

XenApp 6.5 introduces a new server mode, session-only, for servers that only host published applications as shown in the following screenshot:

Choosing the session-host mode only during server setup

Virtual versus physical servers

You can run your XenApp farm on physical servers or on virtual servers.

Citrix supports XenApp running on the following hypervisors:

- Citrix XenServer
- Microsoft Hyper-V
- VMware ESXi

My suggestion is to deploy your farm in a virtual environment; the use of a virtual environment makes possible to deploy new servers in minutes, without the need of buying physical hardware. In the design phase, this means you may choose to split the components on different servers and you may count on the high-availability features of the hypervisor. When the farm is in production, this means you may more easily deploy new servers to fulfill new business requirements or to improve performances.

Sizing controllers

A XenApp farm requires some infrastructure components that run on servers deployed with the controller role. Depending on the size of your farm, you may choose to install all these components on the same server or to scale them on different servers.

Data store

The data store is the repository for all the static information of your farm (farm, servers and applications configurations, administrative accounts, and so on).

Each session-host server in your farm needs a constant connection to the data store. When the **Independent Management Architecture** (**IMA**) service starts, it queries the data store and stores the farm configuration in the **local host cache** (**LHC**). Every 30 minutes, the IMA service then contacts the data store to ensure that its LHC is consistent.

If you deploy your session-host servers specifying the session-only mode, you may reduce the data store load and make the startup and join processes faster, as they require less data during the join and sync process.

 Refer to Citrix Knowledge Base (http://support.citrix. com/article/CTX114501) for the list of supported databases by different Citrix products.

During the setup wizard, you are asked to choose a database. You can choose **New database** to install a local instance of SQL Server Express or **Existing Microsoft SQL Server database** to use a database server already present on your network.

The free SQL Server Express is suitable for small (< 100 servers) farms, while for bigger farms I strongly suggest the use of an enterprise-level database server, possibly in a high availability configuration (such as Microsoft Cluster, Oracle RAC). If the data store is unavailable you can't make changes to the configuration of your farm; moreover if servers reboot, the IMA service won't start and they will no longer publish applications.

In both the cases you should not install other components on the servers that run your database.

XenApp does not usually require much storage for the database. A typical storage requirement is as follows:

Number of servers	Number of applications	Database size
10	50	50 MB
100	250	140 MB
1000	1000	500 MB

Data collector

The data collector manages all the dynamic information of your farm (active and disconnected sessions, server loads, and so on). It also performs resolutions, that is, when a user requires an application, the data collector finds the least loaded server that can run that application.

It is, therefore, a key component in the application startup process. A slowness in the resolution process increases the overall time a user has to wait before the requested application is launched.

You need one data collector for each zone in your farm. A zone is a configurable grouping of XenApp servers; a farm requires at least one zone and all your servers must belong to a zone.

The main purpose to configure zones is to create a hierarchical structure to efficiently distribute changes:

- Servers in a zone notify changes to the data collector of that zone using high-speed links (LAN)
- The data collector then replicates those changes to data collectors of the other zones, usually through slow-speed links (WAN)

Zones are useful in a geographically distributed topology; for example, when your company has more than one site connected with WAN links. Zones are not necessary to divide servers in the same site. I worked with XenApp farms with more than 500 servers in one zone.

Citrix recommends keeping the number of zones in your farm to a minimum with one being optimal. Every time a dynamic event occurs, indeed the data collector of that zone must forward the event to the data collectors of the other zones: this replication consumes CPU and bandwidth.

The following figure is a flowchart by Citrix that helps to decide how many zones you need to deploy:

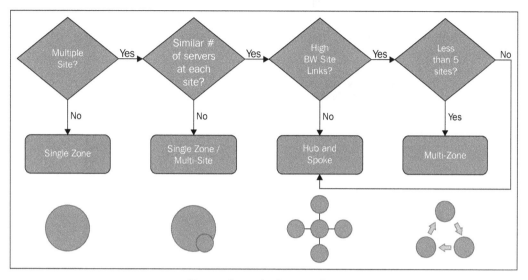

How to choose the farm topology

Data collector stores the entire event in the RAM memory. Its consumption depends on the farm size (number of servers, applications, and so on) and usage (number of active sessions and so on). However, this is usually not significant; for example, a data collector in a large farm (about 500 servers) I administer, uses an average of 250 MB of memory. Similarly, CPU usage is not significant. It may increase only if you create several zones in your farm but this is a discouraged practice. Anyhow, I strongly suggest you to dedicate one server to act as the zone data collector; if the data collector is running on a server that also publishes applications, it may experience resource contention and the resolution process may slow down.

Farms choose the data collector for each zone with an election between all the servers in the zone thatcan run the component (session-host only servers are excluded). XenApp administrators may change the election preference for each server to statically choose which server will be the data collector for the zone. The following screenshot displays the election preference options for the data collector:

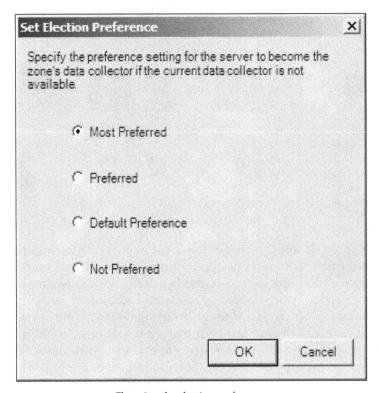

Changing the election preference

Set the election preference to **Most Preferred** only on the dedicated server to be sure it will be chosen as the data collector during the election process.

If the data collector becomes unavailable, a new election is performed. You may also consider to define the backup server (a second dedicated server or a server running rarely used applications) setting its election preference to **Preferred**. The other servers in the farm should keep the default value (**Default Preference**).

XML Broker

The XML Broker is a component used by the Web Interface to retrieve information about the published applications. When a user logs on to the Web Interface, it displays the list of applications retrieved from the XML service to the user. When the user selects an application, the XML Broker responds with the address of a server running that application.

As the XML Broker works closely with the data collector, it is recommended that you install the XML Broker on the same server running the data collector component. If you add more XML Broker servers, you can configure the Web Interface or add an external load balancer (for example, a Citrix NetScaler) to balance the requests between them. The following screenshot displays the option of selecting an XML Broker server for load balancing:

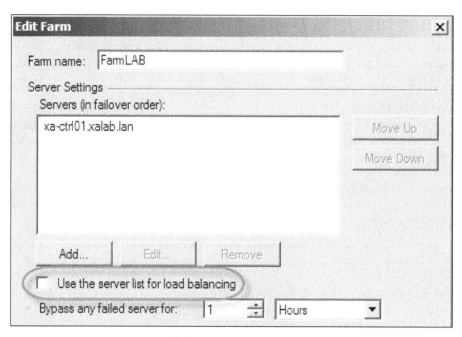

Load balancing XML Broker servers

License server

The license server stores and manages Citrix licenses. The first time a user connects to a XenApp server, the server checks out a license for the user. Subsequent connections of the same user share the same license.

A single license server is enough for farms with thousands of servers and users; you could install a second license server in your farm but the two servers cannot share licenses. Because the license server is contacted when the user connects to a XenApp server, slow responses may increase the login time. You should place the license service on a dedicated server or, in case of small farms, on a server that doesn't publish applications. The license server process is single-threaded so multiple processors do not increase its performance.

If the license server is not available, all the servers in your farm enter a grace period of 720 hours; during this period users are still allowed to connect. This means that you usually don't need a high-availability solution for your license server. If a server fault occurs, you can install a new license server during the 30 days of the grace period or power on a second license server you prepared and kept turned off (cold standby).

Web Interface

The Web Interface provides users access to the published application through a web browser. It's an application running on IIS 7 Web Server and developed in Java/.NET.

A single Web Interface, running on a Dual Core Xeon Server, can handle up to 7 to 8 requests per second. You should expect many connections to the Web Interface when the users arrive at work in the morning or after lunch, so size your Web Interface server based on the number of users you expect will log on at the same time.

A tip to provide high availability and load balancing for this component is to deploy two Web Interface servers and balance the incoming connections using an external HTTP load balancer, as shown in the following diagram:

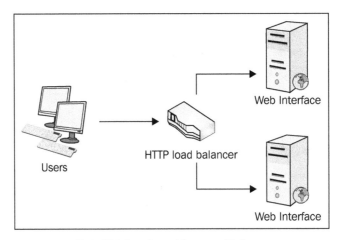

Citrix Web Interface with external balancer

Sizing session hosts

Session host servers publish and run the applications in your farm. Correctly sizing these servers is one of the most critical tasks during the design of your infrastructure; if you underestimate the servers, users will eventually complain about application slowness or worse, some users won't be able to run them at all. If you overestimate them, your boss will probably complain about the cost of the project.

The number of servers you need and their hardware configuration depends on the number of users and applications, but even more on the kind of the applications and how you deliver them to the users. My suggestion is to set up a test farm and to use it to verify the load each application produces. Later in this chapter you'll learn how to use Citrix EdgeSight for Load Testing to simulate real users.

Application delivery methods

Citrix XenApp supports five ways to deliver applications to the users. Each method has pros and cons and the choice of one or another highly changes the resource requirements of the session host servers. The methods are explained in the following sections:

Installed on the server

Applications are installed on the server. When a user launches an application, it runs on the server. Session host servers, therefore, require sufficient resources (CPU and RAM) for the applications, while user devices may be lightweight devices (thin clients, tablets, and smartphones). No offline access is possible.

Streamed to server

Applications are put in profiles and stored on a file or web server. When a user launches an application, this streams to the server where the execution takes place. Session host servers still require sufficient resources (CPU and RAM) for the applications, while user devices don't. No offline access is possible.

Streamed to desktop

Applications are put in profiles and stored on a file or web server. When a user launches an application, this streams to the user device. This device must have enough resources to run the application and must run Windows OS. Applications are cached on the user device, so offline access is possible.

Dual mode delivery

Applications are put in profiles and stored on a file or web server. When a user launches an application, XenApp tries to stream it to the user device. If this is not possible – the device runs an unsupported OS – the application is streamed to the server. This is a more versatile method, but session host servers still require sufficient resources to run the applications in the backup mode.

Applications on servers – siloed versus nonsiloed

The traditional and most common method to deliver applications is to install them on the session host servers. Two strategies available for placing applications on servers are: siloed and nonsiloed.

Siloed

In this approach applications are installed on small groups of servers; you could even have servers running a single application. Applications are usually grouped by their use, for example, all the applications used by the Financial department are installed on the same servers, while the applications used by the HR department are installed on different servers.

This approach is sometimes required if your applications have different hardware requirements or may cause conflicts if installed on the same server. Some application vendors, moreover, don't consider a different licensing if their applications are published through XenApp. So if you pay license fees simply counting the number of installations, you may reduce the cost of installing them on a small number of servers.

Nonsiloed

In this approach all the applications are installed on all the servers. This approach is more efficient as it reduces the number of required servers and it may also improve the user experience because it allows users to share the same server session with different applications. If you're using Provisioning Services, a nonsiloed approach also helps you to reduce the number of different vDisks you have to create and maintain.

My suggestion is to use the nonsiloed approach when possible. Later in this book you'll learn that, with worker groups, you will still be able to logically group applications on servers even with this approach.

Provisioning Services

The Provisioning Services infrastructure allows computers to be provisioned from a single shared image. This technology is widely used in XenDesktop, the desktop virtualization product by Citrix. System administrators prepare a small pool of images and, using Provisioning Services, deploy them to the users. Provisioning Services also becomes very helpful in a XenApp infrastructure, when you need to deploy several session host servers.

The use of this technology offers many benefits. With Provisioning Services, system administrators create and maintain a small number of images (or a single image if all the applications are installed on all the servers) for their servers. If a new application has to be published or an update for an installed application is available, the administrator only has to modify the "master" image and when servers reboot, the change will be deployed on every farm. Server consistency is so assured that there's no risk that some of your servers weren't updated or still run the older version of the application. You may also perform a test of the new image assigning it to a couple of test servers and, if everything is ok, deploy it to the production servers.

If something goes wrong (the updated application doesn't work, an installed patch conflicts with some other component, and so on) and you kept the previous version of the image, a rollback is very easy. Just assign the old image to your servers and reboot them.

Provisioning Services also help to reduce storage costs. The image is streamed via network from a central repository; a local storage is usually required for runtime data caching, but in some scenarios you can remove it entirely.

The use of Provisioning Services certainly requires some more effort during the installation phase, but from my experience I suggest you to consider using this feature if your farm has more than 5 to 10 servers. The time you spend to deploy the Provisioning Services infrastructure is less than the time you would spend for the daily tasks to maintain your farm. In the following sections, you will learn the key concepts of this technology; for a real implementation, please refer to the Citrix documentation.

Provisioning Services infrastructure

The Provisioning Services infrastructure is composed by several components.

At a minimum, you need:

- A license server; it could be the same license server in your XenApp farm.
- A database; you can place Provisioning Services database on the same database server that hosts your farm's data store.
- One or more Provisioning Servers; these run stream services, the software used to stream virtual images to provisioned servers.
- A store, where the images of your servers are saved. You can place the store on the Provisioning Servers or on an external file server.

The following diagram displays the Provisioning Services infrastructure:

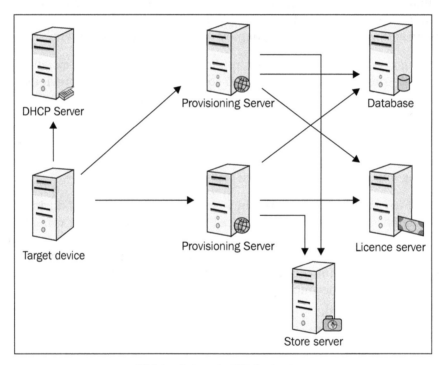

High level view of a PS infrastructure

Infrastructure hierarchy

A Provisioning Services infrastructure is logically divided into a hierarchy of items.

When you install your first **Provisioning Server** (**PVS**), a new farm is created. Do not confuse this farm with the farm of your XenApp infrastructure; they don't share configurations or items. A Provisioning Services farm may serve more XenApp and XenDesktop farms.

A farm contains three major components:

- Sites
- Views
- Stores

Sites

Provisioning Services sites allow administrators to logically group items that belong to the same physical site (for example, all the resources located in the headquarters or in a branch office). You need at least one site, which is created when you install your first Provisioning Server. Administrators may create different sites to delegate administrative tasks. You can indeed create accounts that can only administer items in a given site.

A site contains some elements, the most important of them are:

- **Servers**: The Provisioning Servers in that site.
- **vDisk Pools**: The collection of vDisks (images) available for that site.
- **Device collections**: Logical groups of target devices.

Views

A target device belongs to one device collection. Views provide an alternative method for grouping and managing target devices; a target device may indeed belong to different views. You can create views at farm level or at site level; a view at site level may only contain devices from the same site, while views at farm level may contain all the target devices in that farm.

You can perform some administrative tasks at view level, so views become useful with a large number of target devices. For example, you can reboot all the session host servers that publish an application adding them to a view and issuing the **Restart...** command at the view folder.

Stores

A store is a storage location where you save your vDisks. It may be a local hard disk or a network share.

vDisks

vDisks are disk image files. They consist of a `.vhd` file (contains the data of the virtual disk), any properties files (`.pvp`, contain disk geometry, and configuration), and, if applicable, a chain of differencing disks (`.avhd`).

vDisks may be configured in the following two modes:

- Private image mode; used by a single target device with read/write access
- Shared image mode; shared between multiple devices with read-only access

In shared image mode, target devices can only read the content of the vDisk. Write requests can be cached in four different ways as follows:

Cache on device hard drive

In cache on device hard drive option, write requests are cached on a local hard drive of the target. This is the most common setup, as it frees up the Provisioning Server and doesn't require a large amount of RAM memory. Target servers must have a local hard drive.

Cache in device RAM

In cache in device RAM option, write requests are cached in the target device's memory. This is the fastest method for caching but consumes memory of the target device, reducing the total memory available for running applications.

Cache on a server

In cache on a server option, write requests are handled by the Provisioning Server and cached on a temporary file; in the Store properties you can set the location of these files. This method should be used only if the target device doesn't have a local storage because it increases the network usage and the Provisioning Server load.

Cache on a server persistent

All the previous options are volatile; write cache is lost when the target device reboots. With the cache on a server persistent option, you can set the cache file to be persistent: Provisioning Server creates a cache file for each target device and doesn't clean it if the target reboots. A drawback is that any changes to the original vDisk invalidate all the cache files.

Invalid cache files are not automatically deleted. Remember to periodically check if any exist and manually delete them to free some space.

The following screenshot displays the different ways of caching write requests to disks:

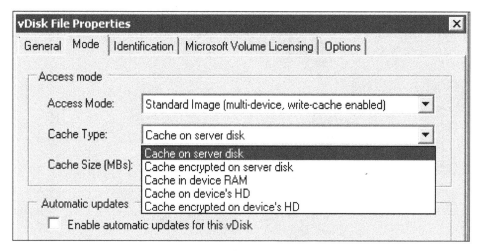

vDisk modes

The boot process

When a target device boots, it first needs a bootstrap program, a small software that runs before the operating system. Provisioning Services use a particular bootstrap program to set up the streaming session with a Provisioning Server. Through this session the target device is then able to receive the assigned vDisk and boot the operating system.

Provisioning Services supports three ways to send the bootstrap program to a target device:

- **Dynamic Host Configuration Protocol (DHCP)**
- **Preboot eXecution Environment (PXE)**
- Boot device stored on attached media

The most common configuration is the use of a DHCP server. You can configure an existing DHCP server in your network or use the DHCP server provided with the Provisioning Server.

The boot process in this scenario is performed in the following three steps:

1. The target device requests an IP address from the DHCP server. The response includes the scope options 66 and 67 with the name and the location of the bootstrap file.

2. Using **Trivial File Transfer Protocol (TFTP)**, the target device requests the bootstrap file from the Provisioning Server. This downloads it to the target.

3. The target device establishes a stream session with the Provisioning Server and boots the assigned vDisk.

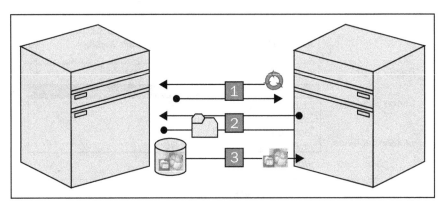

Boot steps of a target device

As an alternative to network booting, you can use Citrix Boot Device Manager to create a bootstrap file on a USB flash device or a CDROM.

Using PVS with XenApp

Begin by building a XenApp master server. A best practice is to choose the session-host only mode during the XenApp installation. Join the server to your farm or use the wizard to create a new farm if this is the first server you deploy. Install all the needed applications and publish them to your users.

Launch the Citrix XenApp Server Role Manager, select **Edit Configuration | Prepare this server for imaging and provisioning** as shown in the following screenshot:

Choose a task to perform

 Prepare this server for imaging and provisioning
This prepares the server for use with system imaging or provisioning tools.

Preparing the server for imaging and provisioning

Choose to remove the server from the farm but don't choose to clear the database location unless you plan to create an Active Directory policy to configure it.

Now, install the Provisioning Services Target Device software. At the end of the setup, the Imaging Wizard should start automatically. If not, run it from the Provisioning Services folder in the Start menu.

First, you need to connect to your PVS farm; enter the name (or the IP address) of one of the servers in your farm and the network port. If you're running the wizard with a user that can administer the farm, choose to use the Windows credentials, otherwise enter the appropriate credentials.

PVS can configure and manage Windows licensing. Choose the licensing method (none, KMS, or MAK) you deployed in your infrastructure.

The Imaging Wizard can create a new vDisk for you; as an alternative, if you've previously created an empty vDisk, you can choose it.

The final step is to create a target device in your PVS farm that corresponds to the server you're running the wizard on. Select the name of the device, the MAC address associated with the NIC you chose during the installation of the target device software, and the collection to add the device to.

Review the information, then click on **Finish** to start the conversion process. After some minutes your vDisk will be ready to use; just remember to change the access mode to **Standard image** before booting new servers with it.

You can manually create new session host servers (for example, from the vSphere client if you're on a VMware infrastructure) or use the Streamed VM Setup wizard from the PVS console to create your servers at once. The wizard supports XenServer, Microsoft Hyper-V, and VMware vSphere.

If you need to modify the vDisk, make a copy, change the mode to **Private**, and assign it to a server. Boot the server, perform the changes, and before shutting it down, remember to launch the Prepare server again for the imaging and provisioning wizard.

Performing load tests with EdgeSight for Load Testing

Citrix offers a complete solution to perform load tests in XenApp and XenDesktop environments: Citrix EdgeSight for Load Testing.

This product is available on the Citrix website; at the moment I'm writing the latest version, 3.8.1.

 You need a valid XenApp license to download and run the product. It's included in the Enterprise or Platinum version

Using EdgeSight for Load Testing, you are able to simulate real user sessions to analyze how your farm performs with different loads; it's a very helpful tool to correctly design your infrastructure.

EdgeSight for Load Testing has two components:

- The **Controller**; used to design and configure test plans and coordinate the launchers during the test execution
- One or more **Launchers;** that receive commands from the controller, create ICA sessions to the target hosts, and replay the test plan, simulating user actions

The following screenshot displays the EdgeSight for Load Testing components:

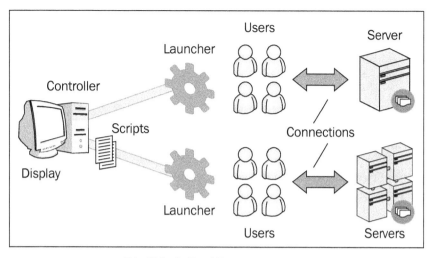

EdgeSight for Load Testing components

Session-host server requirements

You need to change the remote desktop services configuration on the session host servers on which load tests will be applied, using the **Remote Desktop Session Host Configuration** tool.

Ending sessions automatically

No disconnected sessions must remain when virtual users disconnect from servers. Select **ICA-TCP connection** and select **End session** as shown in the following screenshot:

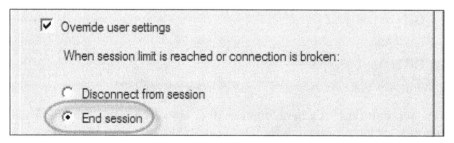

Ending sessions automatically

User session limit

If you're going to use multiple copies of the same virtual users to perform your test, you need to remove the limit of one session per user, and change the **Restrict each user to a single session** setting to **No**.

Web Interface server requirements

It's very common to use the Citrix Web Interface to provide users a portal where they may view and run their applications. If you want to test this component with EdgeSight, you need to install on the server an optional component named Web Interface Support that hosts the Web Interface, included in the EdgeSight for Load Testing setup package.

Using this component, simulated users will be able to log on to the Web Interface, retrieve the published application you want to test, and run it.

 You need at least Web Interface version 4.5

Installation

You may install both Controller and Launcher on the same test machine, or you may install Launcher on dedicated servers. If you need to simulate a large number of users, the second scenario is preferable; if the test machine is under high load, test results may be mistaken.

The system requirements are as follows:

- 2 GHz or faster CPU
- 1 GB RAM
- 1 GB of free disk space
- Windows Vista, Windows 7, or Windows Server 2003, 2008, or 2008 R2

The Launcher requires ICA Client, version 10 or later for testing XenApp systems and version 12 or later for testing XenDesktop systems.

The Controller must be able to connect to Launchers on port TCP/18747 and to connect to your license server (default port is TCP/27000).

License server

Before being able to run any tests, you need to configure your license server. When a test is performed, the Controller checks for a valid XenApp Enterprise or Platinum license. If a license is found, you can run as many users as required.

Open the Controller, in the toolbar you can find a button to open the **Licensing Server Configuration** dialog, enter the address and the port number of your license server and click on **OK**.

Your first script

A script is a single part of a test; it defines the following:

- The actions (instructions) that will be performed
- The users that will perform the actions
- Where (connections) the actions will be performed
- How many users and how long the test will last (load)

To create a new script, select **Test – Add script...**.

Connecting to the farm

In your script, you need to define how users will connect to your XenApp infrastructure.

Right-click on the **Connections** node and select **Add connection...**; enter the name of the Launcher server from which connections will begin.

If you want to connect to a published desktop, select **Server** and enter the server name in the **Connect To** field.

If you prefer to launch an application through the Citrix Web Interface, select **Web Interface** and click on the **Browse...** button.

Insert the address of the server that hosts the Web Interface. You usually don't need to change the port number (**80** is the default) or **Login and Application Page** addresses (you selected those addresses when you installed the Web Interface Support component). Enter the account details of a user that could connect and click on **Search**.

In the Applications tab, you should see all the applications published for that user, select the application your script will test and click on **Select**.

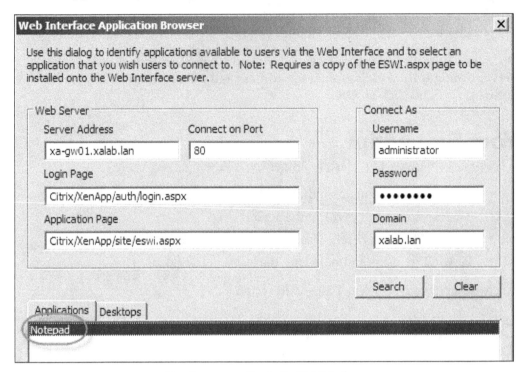

Creating a connection to the Web Interface

Managing users

For each connection you created, you have to define virtual users. Virtual users are used by Launchers to perform the test. You have to create the users, (usually in your Active Directory) and enable them to connect to your farm, and launch the application(s) you want to test.

If you named your test users like:

- testuser1
- testuser2
- testuser3, and so on

with the same password, the **Add Users to Connection** dialog helps you to add them at one time. Enter the number of the users to be added in the **Count** field, then type the base username in the **Username** field and tick the # checkbox.

Complete the **Password** and **Domain** fields and click on **OK**, EdgeSight will add all the users for you as shown in the following screenshot:

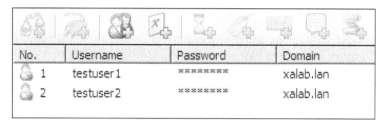

Adding new virtual users

Adding a load

The load defines how long a test will last, how many users will execute it, and at what rate users connect to the server.

If you select the **Concurrency** checkbox, the system attempts to maintain a given number of virtual users during the test, ramping their count between the start and end values.

If you select the **Rate** checkbox, the system attempts to create new virtual users at the rate specified.

Recording instructions

The easiest way to define the actions virtual users will perform is to record them during an interactive session.

You may select the user that will connect to the server by left-clicking on the user's icon or let the system choose the first user for you.

Select the **Instructions** folder and click on the **Record Test** button. The recording session begins and EdgeSight records all the commands you enter. The session ends when you close the connection or if you click on **Stop/Cancel Test** button in the main toolbar. If you stop a recording, you can restart it by clicking on the **Continue** button, while if you cancel it, no instructions are saved.

At the end of the recording, instructions are listed in the **Instructions** folder.

You can change the recorded instructions or add new ones. Instructions are keyboard/mouse commands or even complex Jscript scripts. You can also group instructions in folders and add breakpoints for debugging.

Running a test

When your test plan is ready, you can run it using the **Replay test** button in the main toolbar.

During the test execution, you may watch the virtual users' actions and if you click on the **Display** node, you can get real-time statistics, as shown in the following screenshot:

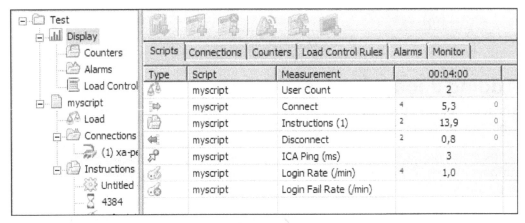

Real-time statistics

Summary

A XenApp infrastructure is made by several components: data store, data collectors, XML brokers, license servers, Web Interface servers, and session-host servers. All contribute to the correct working of the solution. In this chapter, you learned how to correctly size them based on your business requirements.

If you need to deploy several session-host servers, you may consider using Citrix Provisioning Services. With this tool, you can create a master image of your server and use it to provision as many servers as you need. Day-by-day management is also made easier; updates, patches, and changes have to be applied to the master image only.

Even if guidelines and best practices exist, nothing is better than a real test. With EdgeSight for Load Testing, Citrix offers a complete test suite to simulate real loads on a XenApp farm.

2
Monitoring and Improving Server Performances

The XenApp farm you designed is now in production.

The job of a system administrator starts now. The infrastructure must be monitored and maintained. In addition, unpredictable problems in the design phase may appear or new business requirements may arise, increasing the load of your farm.

In this chapter you'll learn:

- How to monitor your XenApp infrastructure
- How to optimize the servers' performance
- Advanced features of XenApp that offers for performance improvement

Health Monitoring & Recovery

Health Monitoring & Recovery (HMR) is a tool included in Citrix XenApp which you can use to run scheduled tests on your servers to monitor their health, and if a problem is detected, you can automatically perform recovery actions.

It includes a standard set of tests, but you can import additional tests downloaded from the Internet or even develop custom ones.

Standard tests

Following are the tests HMR can perform out of the box:

Test name	Description
Citrix IMA Service test	This test checks if the IMA Service is running on the server enumerating the available applications.
Logon monitor test	This test checks if there are many logon/logoff cycles within a short period on the server; this may indicate possible problems in session initialization or application launch.
	You can configure three test parameters specifying the command-line arguments:
	• /SessionTime:sec (default 5 seconds), is the maximum session time for a short logon/logoff cycle
	• /SessionInterval:sec (default 600 seconds), is the time period chosen to monitor logon/logoff cycles
	• /SessionThreshold:cycles (default 50 cycles), is the number of cycles that must occur in the session interval to indicate a test failure
Terminal Services test	This test checks if Windows Terminal Services is running, enumerating list of the sessions on the server.
Ticketing test	This test requires a ticket from the XML Broker service running on the server.
Check DNS test	This test performs a DNS query to obtain the IP address of the server and compares it to the configured address.
	With the /rl flag the test also performs a reverse lookup (retrieves the DNS name from the IP address).
Check LHC test	This test checks the server's Local Host Cache for corrupt or duplicate entries. This is a CPU-intensive check; enable it only if you suspect LHC problems and use a large interval (suggested 86400 seconds = 24 hours).
Check XML Threads test	This test counts the number of worker threads for the XML Broker service. A high number of worker threads could indicate the server is overloaded.
MS Print Spooler test	This checks the Windows Print Spooler Service, enumerating the available printers.
ICA Listener test	This test connects to the local ICA listener to verify if the server is able to accept incoming connections.
Citrix Print Manager Service test	This test checks the Citrix Print Manager Service, enumerating session printers.

Recovery actions

If a test fails, HMR can take one of the following recovery actions:

Recovery action	Description
Alert only	HMR sends an alert to the Event Log.
Prohibit logons and connections to the server	HMR excludes the server from load balancing. Existing connections are maintained and an administrator can still make a direct connection to the server, for example, to troubleshoot the problem.
Shutdown IMA service	HMR stops the IMA service on the server.
Restart IMA service	HMR restarts the IMA service on the server.
Reboot server	HMR reboots the server.

Configuring Health Monitoring & Recovery

HMR is configured via Citrix policies. Three settings are available in Computer policies:

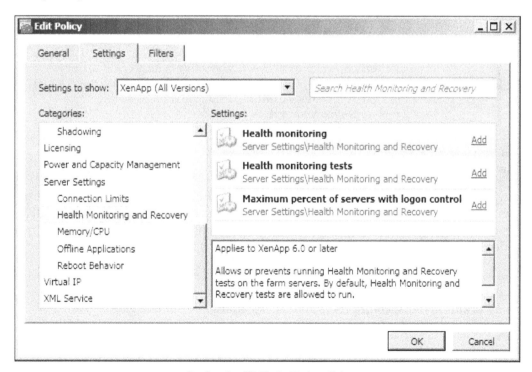

Configuring HMR via Citrix policies

- **Health monitoring**: This lets you enable or disable HMR on the servers the policy applies to

- **Health monitoring tests**: This lets you specify the tests you want HMR to run

- **Maximum percent of servers with logon control**: This lets you control the maximum number of servers. HMR can prohibit logons if you configure this recovery action for some of the tests.

By default, HMR runs on each server of your farm. Not all the available tests apply to both, session-host servers and controllers. Best practice is to have different HMR rules for the two sets of servers to run only the required tests.

Custom tests

You can write your custom tests to be executed by HMR. Test scripts may be:

- Executables
- Command-line scripts (.bat or .cmd)
- Windows scripts (VBScript and JScript)

You can freely download the *Health Monitoring & Recovery SDK* from the Citrix website (http://support.citrix.com/article/ CTX112283). It contains the official documentation, some examples, and a tool for testing your scripts.

Your scripts must be saved under %ProgramFiles(x86)%\Citrix\HealthMon\ Tests\Custom and they will be executed under the LocalService account.

Scripts must issue a known return code to report if the test succeeded or not; a zero return code means success, while a non-zero return code means failure. In the SDK documentation you can find all the available error codes. They match Windows error codes (for example, the return code 2 stands for "file not found").

You're not likely to replace your System Monitoring tool with HMR, but I found the recovery action feature very useful. In a large farm, it helps to immediately isolate non-working servers, before users start complaining.

Using Citrix performance monitoring counters

When you install XenApp on a Windows server, the setup adds some new performance counters you can access from Windows Performance Monitor. A regular analysis of performance data helps to identify possible bottlenecks or lack of free resources.

Citrix performance counters are grouped into six sections. In the next section, you can find a description of the most significant ones.

Citrix CPU Utilization Mgmt User

The following counters are related to the server's CPU:

Counter name	Description
CPU Entitlement	The percentage of CPU resource that Citrix CPU Utilization Management makes available to a user at a given time. You'll learn how to configure CPU Utilization Management later in this chapter.
CPU Reservation	The percentage of CPU resource reserved for a user.
CPU Shares	The proportion of CPU resource assigned to a user.
CPU Usage	The percentage of CPU resource consumed by a user, measured in an interval of a few seconds.
Long-term CPU Usage	The percentage of CPU resource consumed by a user, measured in a longer interval.

Citrix IMA Networking

Three counters are available to monitor IMA service's activity:

Counter name	Description
Bytes Received/sec	Incoming bytes per second
Bytes Sent/sec	Outgoing bytes per second
Network Connections	Number of active IMA connections

Citrix Licensing

Licensing counters measure the time (in milliseconds) of check-in and check-out responses from the License Server.

The License Server Connection Failure counter measures the number of minutes the License Server was unavailable.

Citrix MetaFrame Presentation Server

This section groups counters related to different components of your infrastructure:

Component	Counters
Data store	Statistics about the number of read/write bytes and read/write operations.
Data collector	• Statistics about the resolution process (duration in milliseconds, number of resolutions per second, and so on)
	• Statistics about DynamicStore operations (packets in/out, operations per second, updates to data collectors in different zones, and so on)
	• Statistics about the election process
XML Broker	Number of threads, and number of tickets per second.
Local Host Cache	Statistics about the number of operations per second.

ICA Session

This section contains counters that measure speed, bandwidth, and latency of the different channels in an ICA Session (audio, clipboard, printer, and so on).

Secure Ticket Authority (STA)

This section groups counters about the Secure Ticket Authority service. The STA service is included in the XML Broker service and it's used to control access by the Secure Gateway component.

XenApp on a virtual infrastructure

If you're running your servers on a virtual infrastructure and you're experiencing lack of performance, remember to also check the hypervisor's performance counters. It's common that if the hypervisor is under heavy load, you won't see high CPU values in a virtual machine because the hypervisor can't schedule the virtual CPU on a real CPU.

Using the hypervisor's console, you can inspect the **CPU Ready** counter. It measures the time a **virtual CPU (vCPU)** is ready to run but is not being scheduled on a physical CPU probably because the hypervisor lacks free resources.

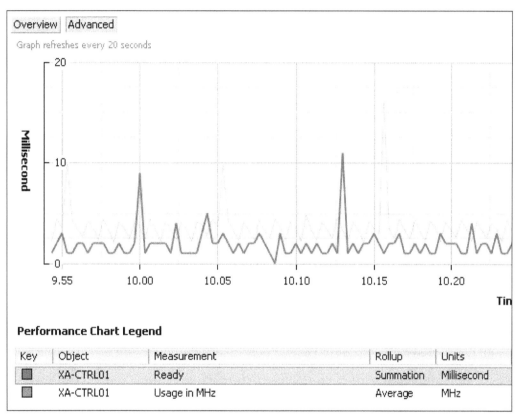

Measuring CPU Ready in VMware

High values of CPU Ready mean that your virtual infrastructure hasn't got enough resources to run all the virtual machines or some of them are producing an abnormal load.

PowerShell SDK

From the Citrix website (`http://community.citrix.com/display/xa/Download+SDKS`), you can download an SDK for Windows PowerShell that allows you to monitor and configure your XenApp farm using PowerShell cmdlets.

This is a very important tool because you can automate some of your administrative tasks, create and schedule health reports, write PowerShell scripts, and integrate them into your monitoring solutions. For example, I've seen many system administrators writing PowerShell scripts to monitor their farms using Nagios, a free monitoring software.

In this and in the following chapters you'll learn some of these PowerShell cmdlets.

> **Remoting**
>
> With XenApp 6.5, Citrix introduced a new feature for its SDK called remoting. With the new SDK you're no longer required to install the SDK on a server. You can install it on a client PC and specify a server as the "target" of your commands using the ComputerName parameter.

CPU Utilization Management

If you're analysing the performance of your farm, in search of possible bottlenecks, you'll most likely find lack of CPU or memory resources.

Citrix CPU Utilization Management is a feature you can enable to improve the way XenApp manages CPU resources and to normalize CPU peaks.

> CPU Utilization Management is a feature included in the Enterprise or Platinum edition of XenApp.

When you enable CPU Utilization Management, the server checks the proportion of CPU resource (share) assigned to each user. By default, it assigns the same share to all the users. This prevents one user that executes CPU-intensive operations from impacting the other users on the same session-host servers.

For example, consider a user who is using a spreadsheet to perform complex financial calculations. Without CPU Utilization Management, his session will probably be consuming most of the CPU resources available on the server, slowing down the work of other connected users. With CPU Utilization Management enabled, instead, his calculations will be slower but other users will be able to work without problems.

Enabling CPU Utilization Management

You can enable CPU Utilization Management with a server policy, using the following setting:

The **Fair sharing of CPU between sessions** setting in **CPU Management server level**.

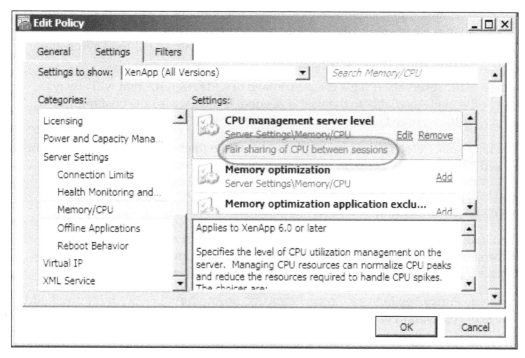

Enabling CPU Utilization Management

Later in this chapter we'll cover the other option available, Preferential Load Balancing.

 CPU Utilization Management is incompatible with Windows Dynamic Fair Share Scheduling. Remember to disable it before enabling CPU Utilization Management!

Shares and reservations

CPU Utilization Management assigns CPU resources based on user shares and reservations:

- **CPU shares:** These are percentage of CPU time. By default a user is allocated four shares. The CPU time a user obtains is proportional to his shares; for example, if a user has two shares and another user has eight, the first user will receive 20 percent of the available CPU time, while the second will receive 80 percent.

- **CPU reservation**: This is a percentage of CPU resource that will always be made available to the user if needed. If the user is not consuming all of the reserved CPU, other users can borrow it.

The range of CPU shares is between 1 and 64, while the total CPU reservation cannot exceed 99 percent.

You learned that, by using Windows Performance Counter, you can access Citrix counters that measure CPU usage, reservation and shares per user.

By default each user is assigned four shares and no reservation. A reservation of 20 percent is guaranteed to the SYSTEM account. You can change the shares for certain users or create reservations through Windows Registry.

Open the **Policy** key in `HKEY_LOCAL_MACHINE\SOFTWARE\Citrix\CTXCPU` and add shares or reservation in the form:

`DOMAIN\user,cpu.shares=#` and `DOMAIN\user,cpu.reservation=#` (percentage in thousands).

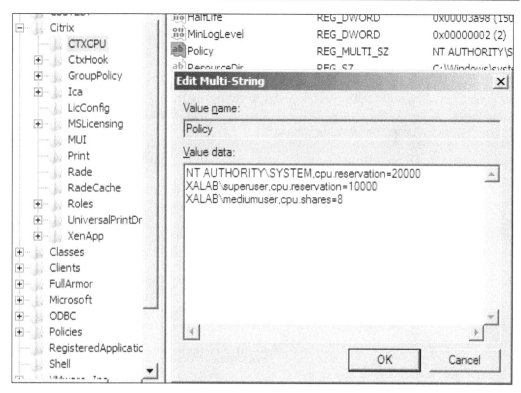

Assigning shares and reservations

Restart the **Citrix CPU Utilization Mgmt/Resource Mgmt** service to apply the new settings.

 You've probably noticed that Citrix CPU Utilization Mgmt/Resource Mgmt service is set to **Manual** startup. That's because the IMA service starts it only when you enable the feature.

Windows Dynamic Fair Share Scheduling

You learned that Citrix CPU Utilization Management is incompatible with Windows **Dynamic Fair Share Scheduling** (DFSS), which is the CPU optimization solution Microsoft included in Remote Desktop Services since Windows 2008 R2.

DFSS uses the kernel-level scheduling mechanism of Windows to distribute processor time across sessions, ensuring that each one does not consume too many resources and does not degrade the performances of the others.

Working with a kernel driver allows DFSS to react instantly when a new session is launched, while Citrix CPU Utilization Management acts upon triggers or on a scheduled basis.

In my experience, Citrix CPU Utilization Management works better with ICA sessions than Microsoft DFSS and it's easier to configure (DFSS requires an additional component, named Windows System Resource Manager, if you need to configure different policies based on users or groups).

You can disable DFSS setting `EnableCpuQuota` to `0` in the following registry key

`HKLM\SYSTEM\CurrentControlSet\Control\Session Manager\Quota System\`
or via a group policy as shown in the following screenshot:

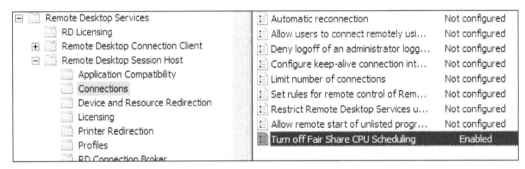

Using Group Policy to disable DFSS

High CPU load on datastore

If your data store server suffers high CPU load, you can increase the polling interval at which each server in your farm queries the data store to retrieve new changes.
If you notice high CPU load on the server that runs your data store, you may adjust the interval each server in your farm queries the data store for syncing new changes.

The default interval is 30 minutes and you can increase it with the `DCNChangePollingInterval` DWORD value in the registry key:

`HKEY_LOCAL_MACHINE\SOFTWARE\Wow6432Node\Citrix\IMA`.

The value must be expressed in milliseconds and you need to restart the IMA Service to apply the change.

Memory optimization

Each session consumes part of the available memory on your server. If the memory request exceeds the available memory, the operating system needs to swap some of the RAM memory to disk, degrading the overall performance of the server.

The memory optimization feature can reduce the memory utilization improving DLL-sharing among applications.

DLL collisions

A **Dynamic Link Library (DLL)** is a library that contains code, data, and resources. It can be used by different programs at the same time. By using DLLs, applications can be modularized and can also include third-party libraries. DLLs promote code reuse and reduce the load time of the program because they are loaded into memory when requested.

Every DLL has a **preferred base address**, which is the memory address where the module should be mapped into the process' address space (virtual memory)by the operating system.

If two DLLs have the same preferred base address, when the OS loads them into memory, a **collision** occurs as shown in the following screenshot:

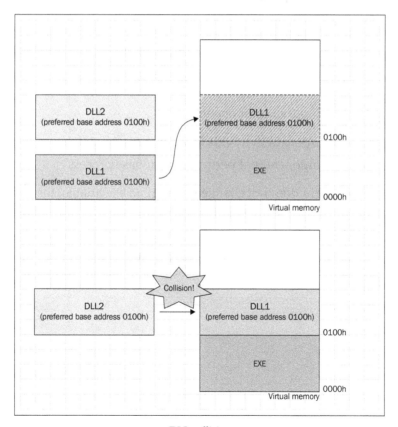

DLL collision

When a collision occurs, the OS has to relocate the DLL to a different address available and the relocated DLL cannot be shared by different applications.

Relocating a DLL has two drawbacks:

- The DLL cannot be shared, consuming more RAM memory
- The OS has to update the executable file, slowing application start-up

DLL rebasing and binding

Memory optimization avoids DLL collisions changing the preferred base address of the DLLs that may cause collision. This process is called **rebasing**.

This feature may also speed up applications, binding the DLLs to the executables. Usually, when an application calls a function exported by a DLL, it needs to look at the export table of that DLL. Memory optimization modifies the executable to statically bind the memory address of these functions so the application can call the functions without the need to read the export table.

 Not all the executables work with rebasing and binding. Test all your applications in a test environment before enabling memory optimization in your production farm!

Memory optimization has two components:

- A **scanning** component that finds DLLs that are candidates to be rebased
- A **rewriting** component that performs the rebase process

The rewriting component does not change the original executable. Instead it creates a new copy and includes changes, if any, and sets this copy as an alternate data stream of the original one.

A file filter driver, installed by XenApp, intercepts calls to the filesystem, and if a file has an alternate data stream, it sends this to the OS in place of the original one.

Configuring Memory optimization

The memory optimization feature is controlled by Citrix Computer policies.

The available settings in the Memory/CPU category are:

Setting	Description
Memory optimization	Enables or disables the Memory optimization feature
Memory optimization application exclusion list	Lists the applications that Memory optimization should not rebase
Memory optimization interval	Specifies the interval for running the optimization process
Memory optimization schedule: day of month	If the interval is set to **Monthly,** it specifies the day of month to run the optimization process
Memory optimization schedule: day of week	If the interval is set to **Weekly,** it specifies the day of week to run the optimization process
Memory optimization schedule: time	If the interval is set to **Monthly, Weekly,** or **Daily,** it specifies the time of day to run the optimization process

If you create specific Computer policies, you can enable memory optimization only on some servers of your farm.

 If Memory optimization is enabled, it always runs at server startup. Using the previous settings you can add a new schedule but you can't change or disable the default one.

Excluding applications

Not all the applications can be rebased. Memory optimization is able to detect and automatically exclude:

- The applications saved on network drives
- The applications with digitally signed components
- The applications with DLLs protected by Windows Rights Management

Memory optimization is not able to detect and exclude applications that require DLLs with fixed addresses or applications that check the DLLs after the OS loads them into memory. You have to manually exclude these applications adding their executables in the **Memory optimization application exclusion list** as shown in the following screenshot:

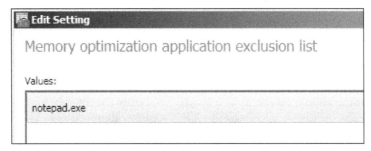

Adding an application to the exclusion list

 If you modify a Citrix policy, you can force the server to refresh the associated policies with the gpupdate command.

The applications included in the exclusion list are added to the following registry key:

HKLM\SOFTWARE\Wow6432Node\Citrix\SFO\ProcessExclusionList.

You cannot exclude a DLL using Citrix policies. You have to manually add the DLL name to the following key:

HKLM\SOFTWARE\Wow6432Node\Citrix\SFO\ComponentExclusionList.

Both the keys include a list of known incompatible executables and components:

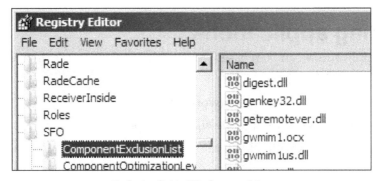

Exclusion list in Windows registry

Troubleshooting

When you enable memory optimization, the IMA Service starts the **Citrix Virtual Memory Optimization** service, which is tied to the scanning component (CtxSFOSvc. exe). This process monitors the OS looking for DLL collisions. When a collision occurs, it writes the DLL name to the Repair.sfo or Repair64.sfo files located in %ProgramFiles(x86)%\Citrix\Server Resource Management\Memory Optimization Management\Data. In the same folder, you can find the logs.

During system startup, if set and when scheduled, the rewriting component (CtxBace.exe) reads those files, optimizes the listed DLLs, and binds the executables to them. A third component, CtxTestDLL.exe, loads the DLL after the optimization to ensure it's still functional.

Using the Citrix PowerShell SDK you can analyze how much memory is saved by Memory optimization:

```
PS C:\> Get-XAMemoryOptimization <serverName>
```

```
PS C:\> Get-XAMemoryOptimization xa-app01

ServerName   ProcessName                              SavingsKB
----------   -----------                              ---------
XA-APP01     C:\PROGRAM FILES (X86)\CIT...                25872
XA-APP01     C:\WINDOWS\MICROSOFT.NET\F...                   48
XA-APP01     C:\PROGRAM FILES (X86)\CIT...                16952
```

OS optimization

Citrix XenApp runs on Windows 2008 R2. It's possible to apply some changes to the OS configuration to increase the overall performances of the server.

A document including all the suggested modifications has been published by Citrix (http://support.citrix.com/article/CTX131577). In the next section I'm listing, in my opinion, the most important ones.

All the servers

The following modifications apply to all the session-host servers in your farm:

Paging system components

You can prevent system components to be paged to disk with the following registry key:

`HKLM\SYSTEM\CurrentControlSet\Control\Session Manager\Memory Management` — `DisablePagingExecutive` = `dword:00000001`

Power saving

Select the maximum performance scheme in both your server BIOS and in Windows Power Plan.

Worker threads

You can increase the number of threads Windows uses for read-ahead and write-behind requests, improving I/O performance:

`HKLM\SYSTEM\CurrentControlSet\Control\Session Manager\Executive` — `AdditionalCriticalWorkerThreads` = `dword:00000064` (decimal).

Page file

You should set your page file with the same minimum and maximum size, so Windows creates the whole page file at startup. A rule of thumb is to set the page file equal to the size of RAM, but some good articles (for example, `http://blogs.citrix.com/2011/12/23/the-pagefile-done-right/`) are available to help a system administrator to properly size the page file based on tests on real workloads.

Provisioned servers

If your session-host servers are provisioned by Provisioning Services, changes to the single server are lost after a reboot so you can safely disable some Windows components and features as discussed in the next section.

System restore

System restore regularly creates and saves restore points of your system. You can disable it via group policy by going to:

Administrative Template | System | System Restore | Turn off System Restore.

Background defragmentation and layout service

You should defragment your disk before capturing the vDisk image; provisioned servers usually don't need periodic defragmentation.

The layout service rearranges files on the hard disks to increase performance.

You can disable both background defragmentation and layout service via Windows registry:

`HKLM\SOFTWARE\Microsoft\Dfrg\BootOptimizeFunction — Enable=N`

`HKLM\SOFTWARE\Microsoft\Windows\CurrentVersion\OptimalLayout — EnableAutoLayout=dword:00000000`

Antivirus

Citrix recommends configuring your antivirus product with the following exclusions:

Name	Note
Network locations	Scanning network locations is usually a slow process. Use a dedicated antivirus product to scan your file servers
Pagefile	Pagefile is used by the OS to swap unused memory pages if the memory request exceeds the available memory
Print spooler folder	`%SystemRoot%\SYSTEM32\SPOOL\PRINTERS` This folder contains the print jobs as they are processed by the OS
Local Host Cache database `Imalhc.mdb`	Saved in `%ProgramFiles(x86)%\Citrix\ Independent Management Architecture`
Application Streaming offline database, `RadeOffline.mdb`	Saved in `%ProgramFiles(x86)%\Citrix\ Independent Management Architecture`
Application Stream cache and deploy folders	`%ProgramFiles(x86)%\Citrix\RadeCache` `%ProgramFiles(x86)%\Citrix\Deploy`

Worker groups

Worker groups are a collection of XenApp servers.

A worker group can contain any number of servers from the same farm it belongs to. It can also be empty. A server can belong to different worker groups.

With worker groups you can:

- Publish an application to a group of servers and decide how to balance incoming requests among them
- Filter Citrix policies so their settings are applied only to specific servers
- Assign the same load evaluator to a group of servers

Creating a worker group

To create a worker group, right-click on the **Worker Groups** node in Citrix AppCenter, and select **Create worker group**.

You need to give a name to the new worker group, an optional description, and select the source of the servers:

- Active Directory Containers
- Active Directory Server Groups
- Farm Servers

A worker group can either be static or dynamic. If you choose **Farm Servers**, you can manually add one or more servers to your farm. Choosing an **Active Directory** option instead lets you "link" the worker group to an Active Directory Organizational Unit or Group. The servers contained in that **Organizational Unit (OU)** or a member of that Group will be automatically added to the worker group. If a new server is added to the OU or Group or a server is removed, the same server is added or removed from the worker group.

 This is a very useful feature combined with Provisioning Services. You can deploy a new server using Provisioning Services and if you publish your applications to worker groups, as soon as the Provisioning Services adds the server to the correct OU, this will start to serve your users.

Publishing applications

When publishing an application, you can choose worker groups from the list of the servers that host the application as shown in the following screenshot:

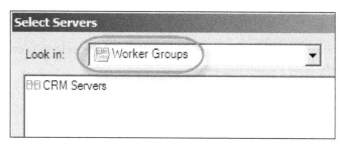

Choosing a worker group when publishing an application

All the servers in the worker group must have the application installed. If the application is missing on any server, Citrix logs an error in the Application event log of the data collector.

With worker groups, you can install all the applications on all your servers (non-siloed approach) but choose, at any time, which of your servers will run any application. Because a server may belong to different worker groups, you are able to balance the load of your farm and dynamically adapt to it.

For example, if the requests for an application have peaks during the day, in those periods you can add (manually or using a PowerShell script) more servers to the worker group, while during the rest of the day these servers publish other applications.

I usually create a single image for all my session-host servers and I do extensively use worker groups to group my servers and load balance the requests. This approach makes the infrastructure very flexible and it's absolutely recommended where possible.

The PowerShell cmdlets to add and remove a list of servers from a workergroup are:

- `Add-XAWorkerGroupServer`
- `Remove-XAWorkerGroupServer`

Load-balancing policies

Using load-balancing policies you can group your users and assign them a list of preferred worker groups. Load-balancing policies are usually implemented to direct users to the closest group of servers (in a multisite environment) to configure "backup" worker groups or simply to direct specific users to dedicated servers.

To create a new policy, right-click on the Load Balancing node in Citrix AppCenter and choose **Create load balancing policy**.

Enter a name for the new policy and an optional description.

Apply one or more filters to the users:

- **Access Control**: It lets you filter the users based on "how" they connect to the farm (through Access Gateway or not).

- **Client IP address**: It lets you filter the users based on their IP addresses; you can enter a list of IP addresses, IP ranges or IP subnets.

- **Client Name**: It lets you filter the users based on the name of their clients. This filter doesn't work if your users connect using the Web Interface.

- **Users**: It lets you filter the users based on their username or group membership.

[You must configure at least one filter; otherwise the policy won't be applied.]

Enter the list of the worker groups this policy will apply to; you can increase or decrease their priority (1 is the highest):

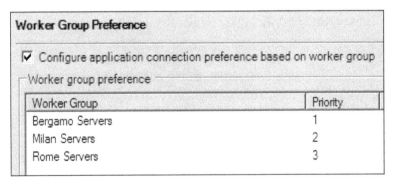

Configuring worker group preference

When a user launches an application, XenApp directs the user to one of the servers in the worker group with the highest priority. Only if all the servers in this worker group are full or offline, XenApp chooses a server from the worker group with lower priority.

XenApp chooses the server within a worker group using the resolution process you learned to be executed by the data collector.

Policies also have a priority. If a user matches multiple policies, XenApp chooses the one with highest priority. You can change the priority of a policy from the **context** menu or from the **Actions** pane as shown in the following screenshot:

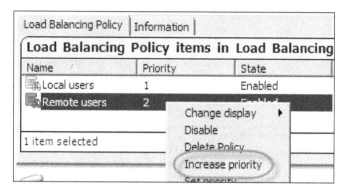

Changing the priority of a policy

Load evaluators

You learned that during the resolution process, the data collector chooses the least loaded server to launch the requested application. How can it determine the load level for each server?

XenApp calculates the load on a server using **load evaluators.** Each server must have one and only one load evaluator assigned to it. You can also attach a load evaluator to a single application.

 If you assign a load evaluator to both a server and an application on it, XenApp will choose the evaluator that reports the highest load.

Each load evaluator contains one or more rules. A rule defines an operational range for the server or the published application. When any rule reports full load or exceeds its threshold, XenApp considers the server unavailable and removes it from the list of balanced servers. When all the rules return values below the configured thresholds, the server is added to the list again.

Load rules

A load evaluator can contain one or more of the following rules:

Rule name	Code	Description
Application User Load	a	Monitors the number of users accessing a specific application.
		You can configure the number of users to report full load (default 100) and the application name.
Context Switches	2	Monitors the number of context switches per second; a context switch occurs when the OS switches from one process to another.
		You can configure two thresholds: the number of context switches per second to report full load and the number to report no load.
CPU Utilization	1	Monitors the percentage of CPU utilization.
		You can configure two thresholds: the percentage of CPU utilization to report full load and the percentage to report no load.
Disk Data I/O	7	Monitors the disk I/O throughput in kilobytes per second.
		You can configure two thresholds: the throughput to report full load and the throughput to report no load.
Disk Operations	8	Monitors the number of disk operations per second (IOPS).
		You can configure two thresholds: the number of operations to report full load and the number of operations to report no load.
IP Range	9	Does not evaluate the load and must be used in conjunction with another rule. It allows defining a range of allowed or denied IP addresses for a published application.

Rule name	Code	Description
Load Throttling	d	Defines how user logons impact server performance. The logon process in fact loads a server significantly. With this rule, you can prevent users from bringing the server down with many concurrent logons.
		You can choose between five levels from medium low to extreme.
Memory Usage	3	Monitors the percentage of memory utilization.
		You can configure two thresholds: the percentage of memory utilization to report full load and the percentage to report no load.
Page Faults	4	Monitors the number of page faults per second; a page fault occurs when the OS needs to read a page of memory that was swapped to disk.
		You can configure two thresholds: the number of page faults per second to report full load and the number of page faults to report no load.
Page Swaps	6	Monitors the number of page swaps per second; a page swap occurs when the OS needs to swap a page of memory to disk.
		You can configure two thresholds: the number of page swaps per second to report full load and the number of page swaps to report no load.
Scheduling	5	Configures the availability of servers or applications.
		You can schedule different intervals with different time ranges.
Server User Load	b	Monitors the number of active users on the server.
		You can configure the number of users to report full load (default 100).

Default load evaluator

When you add a server to your farm, XenApp assigns a **default** load evaluator. This contains two rules:

- Server User Load, configured with a threshold of 100 users.
- Load Throttling, configured as high impact.

An Advanced load evaluator is also available out of the box. It contains CPU Utilization Load, Memory Usage, Page Swaps, and Load Throttling rules, all with default values.

Creating and assigning a load evaluator

To create a new load evaluator, right-click on the Load Evaluators node in Citrix AppCenter and choose **New | Add load evaluator**:

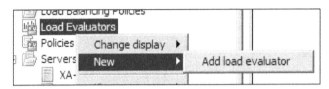

Creating a new load evaluator

Give a name to the new load evaluator, an optional description and choose one or more rules. For each rule, you can change the default thresholds or settings.

You can assign load evaluators to servers or worker groups using Citrix policies.

Create a new server policy or edit an existing one and change the **Load Evaluator Name** setting:

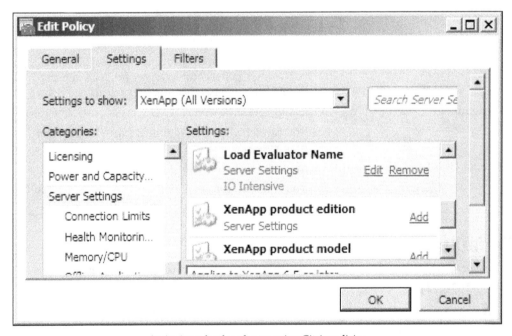

Assigning a load evaluator using Citrix policies

You can assign the chosen load evaluator, filtering the configured policy to a specific server or worker group.

To assign a load evaluator to an application, right-click on the application and choose
Other Tasks | Attach application to load evaluator:

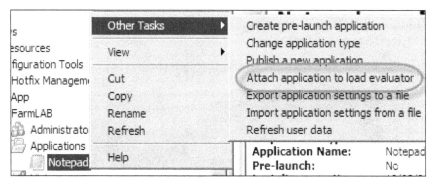

Assigning a load evaluator to an application

Analyzing load evaluators

With the help of Citrix PowerShell SDK, you can analyse the load of your servers
using the Get-XAServerLoad cmdlet:

```
PS C:\> Get-XAServerLoad
```

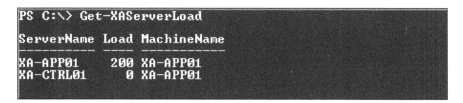

The cmdlet returns, for all the servers in your farm, the load value reported by the
load evaluator assigned to them. You can also filter the output to obtain the load of
a single server using the ServerName parameter. This is useful, for example, if you're
writing a script to check if a server is overloaded (a load value of 10,000 means the
server is fully loaded).

With the previous cmdlet, you cannot analyze "how" the load value was calculated by
the load evaluator, that is, which rules were applied and their weight in the total value.

To analyze the single rules, you need a different tool such as QueryDS that is
available under \Support\debug of the XenApp installation DVD.

With the following command you can obtain the load details of your servers:

```
D:\Support\debug> QueryDS /table:LMS_ServerLoadTable
```

In particular, the line **RuleLoads** reports the load associated with each rule, in the form `rule_number:rule_load`:

```
D:\Support\debug>queryds /table:LMS_ServerLoadTable

[LMS_ServerLoadTable]: 2 records.

name           : 57f6-000c-000001d3
host           : XA-APP01
zone           : Default Zone
RealTimeRules  :
LoadBias       : 64
LTMultiplier   : 2
LogonMode      : 0
PcmMode        : 0
RuleLoads      : d:0;b:2;
Load           : c8
LTLoad         : 0
```

Getting rule loads with QueryDS utility

Values are percentages of 100 in hex notation, while rules are expressed with their code (refer to the load rule evaluator rules to get rule name from the code).

In the example, the actual server load (hex c8 = 200) is caused by a load of 200 (2 x 100) measured by the Server User Load (b) rule.

Preferential Load Balancing

With load evaluators, you can change how XenApp evaluates the load of servers or applications. Load evaluator rules are based on performance indicators (CPU, memory, paging, and so on), not on the importance of your users.

Using **Preferential Load Balancing**, you can assign importance levels (Low, Normal, or High) to users and applications. Users or applications with higher importance level receive more computing resources.

 Preferential Load Balancing is a feature available only with a Platinum license

Preferential Load Balancing calculates the resource allotment for each session, considering both user and application importance levels.

Enabling Preferential Load Balancing

To use Preferential Load Balancing, you first need to enable the feature with a server policy:

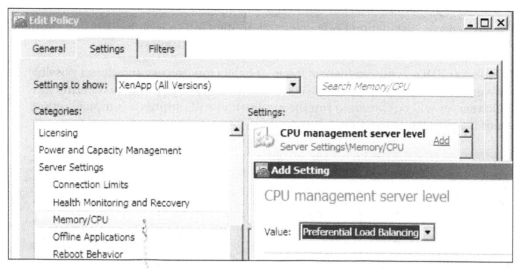

Enabling Preferential Load Balancing

Then, you can change your users' importance with the creation of different user policies:

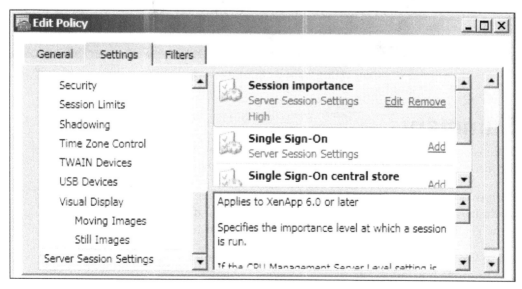

Assigning High importance with user policy

Finally, you can change the importance of a single application in the **Limits** section of the application properties (the setting is visible only if you own a Platinum license).

Testing load balancing

On the XenApp installation DVD you can find the LBDiag tool that lets you simulate the load-balancing process for a user requesting an application.

Thanks to LBDiag, you can inspect the load balancing process and detect possible problems. LBDiag evaluates all the configurations that contribute to determinate which server will be chosen to run the application and outputs a complete report about the process:

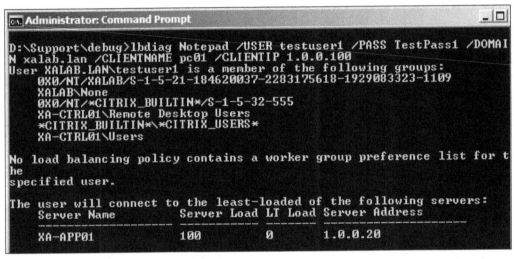

Using LBDiag to analyse the load balancing process

Summary

In this chapter you learned how to monitor your XenApp infrastructure and the most important indicators that may warn you about overloaded servers.

With two XenApp features (CPU Utilization Management and Memory Optimization) you can optimize the usage of CPU and RAM, while changing some Windows settings you can optimize the OS for hosting ICA sessions.

Using Worker groups, Load evaluators and Preferential Load Balancing you can also improve how applications and sessions are balanced on your servers, with the ability to configure different importance levels for users and applications.

3
Optimizing Session Startup

The most frequent complaint that system administrators receive from users about XenApp is definitely that the applications start slowly. They certainly do not consider that at least the first time you launch an application published by XenApp, an entire login process takes place.

In this chapter you'll learn:

- Which steps form the login process and which systems are involved
- The most common causes of logon delays and how to mitigate them
- The use of some advanced XenApp features, like session pre-launch

The logon process

Let's briefly review the logon process that starts when a user launches an application through the Web Interface or through a link created by the Receiver. Some of the steps have been already presented in *Chapter 1, Designing a Scalable XenApp Infrastructure*, where you learned the different components of a Citrix farm. The following diagram explains the logon process:

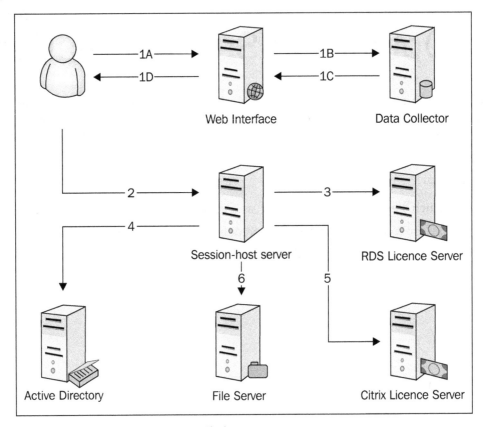

The logon process

Resolution

The user launches an application (A) and the Web Interface queries the Data Collector (B) that returns the least-loaded server for the requested application (C). The Web Interface generates an ICA file and passes it to the client (D).

Connection

The Citrix client running on the user's PC establishes a connection to the session-host server specified in the ICA file. In the handshake process, client and server agree on the security level and capabilities.

Remote Desktop Services (RDS) license

Windows Server validates that an RDS/**Terminal Server** (**TS**) license is available.

AD authentication

Windows Server authenticates the user against the **Active Directory** (**AD**). If the authentication is successful, the server queries account details from the AD, including **Group Policies** (**GPOs**) and roaming profiles.

Citrix license

XenApp validates that a Citrix license is available.

Session startup

If the user has a roaming profile, Windows downloads it from the specified location (usually a file server). Windows then applies any GPOs and XenApp applies any Citrix policies. Windows executes applications included in the **Startup** menu and finally launches the requested application.

 Some other steps may be necessary if other Citrix components (for example, the Citrix Access Gateway) are included in your infrastructure.

Analysing the logon process

Users perceive the overall duration of the process from the time when they click on the icon until the appearance of the application on their desktops. To troubleshoot slowness, a system administrator must know the duration of the individual steps.

Citrix EdgeSight

Citrix EdgeSight is a performance and availability management solution for XenApp and XenDesktop. If you own an Enterprise or Platinum XenApp license, you're entitled to install EdgeSight Basic (for Enterprise licensing) or Advanced (for Platinum licensing). You can also license it as a standalone product.

If you deployed Citrix EdgeSight in your farm, you can run the **Session Startup Duration Detail** report, which includes information on both, the duration of server-side and client-side steps. This report is available only with EdgeSight Advanced.

For each session, you can drill down the report to display information about server-side and client-side startup processes. An example is shown in the following screenshot:

Session Startup Duration Detail

Session Startup Duration Detail for department "All\XenApp Farms"

Session Started	Device	User	Client Address	Client Name	Avg SSD	Avg CSD
3/25/2013 02:30:02 PM	XA-APP01	XALAB\testuser1	1.0.0.100	TESTPC01	17039	

Server Startup Details

Start Time	End Time	CASD	CONSD	PNCOSD	PLSD	LSESD	PCSD	DMSD	SCSD	SSD	
3/25/2013 02:30:03 PM	3/25/2013 02:30:21 PM	15			15790	721		103	410	17039	

Client Startup Details

Start Time	CFDCD	BUCC	AECD	IFDCD	NRWD	TRWD	LPWD	SCCD	NRCD	SLCD	CSD
3/25/2013 02:30:21 PM								6376			

EdgeSight's Session Startup Duration Detail report

The columns report the time (in milliseconds) spent by the startup process in the different steps. **SSD** is the total server-side time, while **CSD** the total client-side time. You can find a full description of the available reports and the meaning of the different acronyms in the EdgeSight Report List at `http://community.citrix.com/display/edgesight/EdgeSight+5.4+Report+List`. In the preceding example most of the time was spent in the **Profile Load (PLSD)** and **Login Script Execution (LSESD)** steps on the server and in the **Session Creation (SCCD)** step on the client.

EdgeSight is a very valuable tool to analyze your farm. The available reports cover all the critical areas and gives detailed information about the "hidden" work of Citrix XenApp.

With the Session Startup Duration Detail report you can identify which steps cause a slow session startup. If you want to understand why server-side steps, like the Profile Load step in the preceding example that lasted more than 15 seconds, take too much time, you need a different tool.

Windows Performance Toolkit

Windows Performance Toolkit (WPT) is a tool included in the Windows ADK, freely downloadable from the Microsoft website (`http://www.microsoft.com/en-us/download/details.aspx?id=30652`).

> You need an Internet connection to install Windows ADK. You can run the setup on a client with Internet access and configure it to download all the required components in a folder. Move the folder on your server and perform an offline installation.

WPT has two components:

- **Windows Performance Recorder**, which is used to record all the performance data in an `.etl` file
- **Windows Performance Analyzer**, a graphical program to analyze the recorded data

Run the following command from the WPT installed folder to capture slow logons:

```
C:\WPT>xperf -on base+latency+dispatcher+NetworkTrace+Registry+File
IO -stackWalk CSwitch+ReadyThread+ThreadCreate+Profile -BufferSize 128
-start UserTrace -on "Microsoft-Windows-Shell-Core+Microsoft-Windows-
Wininit+Microsoft-Windows-Folder Redirection+Microsoft-Windows-User
Profiles Service+Microsoft-Windows-GroupPolicy+Microsoft-Windows-
Winlogon+Microsoft-Windows-Security-Kerberos+Microsoft-Windows-User
Profiles General+e5ba83f6-07d0-46b1-8bc7-7e669a1d31dc+63b530f8-29c9-4880-
a5b4-b8179096e7b8+2f07e2ee-15db-40f1-90ef-9d7ba282188a"  -BufferSize 1024
-MinBuffers 64 -MaxBuffers 128 -MaxFile 1024
```

After having recorded at least one slow logon, run the following command to stop recording and save the performance data to an `.etl` file:

```
C:\WPT>xperf -stop -stop UserTrace -d merged.etl
```

This command creates a file called `merged.etl` in the WPT install folder. You can open this file with Windows Performance Analyzer. The Windows Performance Analyzer timeline is shown in the following screenshot:

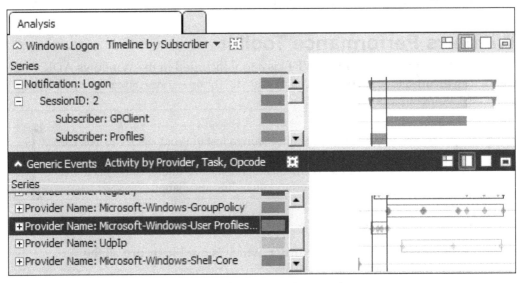

Windows Performance Analyzer timeline

Windows Performance Analyzer shows a timeline with the duration of each step; for any point in time you can view the running processes, the usage of CPU and memory, the number of I/O operations, and the bytes sent or received through the network.

WPT is a great tool to identify the reason for delays in Windows; it, however, has no visibility of Citrix processes. This is why EdgeSight is still necessary for complete troubleshooting.

Common causes of logon delays

After having analyzed many logon problems, I found that the slowness was usually caused by one or more of the following reasons:

- Authentication issues
- Profile issues
- GPO and logon script issues

In the next paragraphs, you'll learn how to identify those issues and how to mitigate them. Even if you can't use the advanced tools (EdgeSight, WPT, and so on) described in the preceding sections, you can follow the guidelines in the next sections and best practices to solve or prevent most of the problems related to the logon process.

Authentication issues

During the logon process, authentication happens at multiple stages; at minimum when a user logs on to the Web Interface and when the session-host server creates a session for launching the requested application. Citrix XenApp integrates with Active Directory. The authentication is therefore performed by a **Domain Controller** (**DC**) server of your domain.

Slowness in the Domain Controller response, caused by an overloaded server, can slow down the entire process. Worse, if the Domain Controller is unavailable, a domain member server may try to connect for 30 seconds before timing out and choosing a different DC.

Domain member servers choose the Domain Controller for authenticating users based on their membership to Active Directory Sites. If sites are not correctly configured or don't reflect the real topology of your network, a domain member server may decide to use a remote Domain Controller, through a slow WAN link, instead of using a Domain Controller on the same LAN.

Profile issues

Each user has a profile that is a collection of personal files and settings. Windows offers different types of profiles, with advantages and disadvantages as shown in the following table:

Type	Description
Local	The profile folder is local to each server.
Roaming	The profile folder is saved on a central storage (usually a file server).
Mandatory	A read-only profile is assigned to users; changes are not saved across sessions.

From the administrator's point of view, mandatory profiles are the best option because they are simple to maintain, allow fast logon, and users can't modify Windows or application settings. This option however is not often feasible. I could use mandatory profiles only in specific cases, for example; when users have to run only a single application without the need to customize it.

Local profiles are almost never used in a XenApp environment because even if they offer the fastest logon time, they are not consistent across servers and sessions. Furthermore, you'll end up with all your session-host servers storing local profiles for all your users, and that is a waste of disk space. Finally, if you're provisioning your servers with Provisioning Server, this option, if not applicable as local profiles. would be saved in the local cache, which is deleted every time the server reboots.

System administrators usually choose roaming profiles for their users. Roaming profiles indeed allow consistency across servers and sessions and preserve user settings and changes.

Roaming profiles are, however, the most significant cause of slow logons. Without a continuous control, they can rapidly grow to a large size. A small profile with a large number of files, for example, a profile with many cookies, can cause delays too.

Roaming profiles also suffer of the **last write wins** problem. In a distributed environment like a XenApp farm, it is not unlikely that users are connected to different servers at the same time. Profiles are updated when users log off, so with different sessions on different servers, some settings could be overwritten, or worse, the profile could be corrupted.

Folder redirection

To reduce the size of roaming profiles, you can redirect most of the user folders to a different location. Instead of saving files in the user's profile, you can configure Windows to save them on a file sharing system.

The advantages of using folder redirection are:

* The data in the redirected folders is not included in the synchronization job of the roaming profile, making the user logon and logoff processes faster
* Using disk quotas and redirecting folders to different disks, you can limit how much space is taken up by single folders instead of the whole profile

- Windows Offline Files technology allows users to access their files even when no network connection is available
- You can redirect some folders (for example, the Start Menu) to a read-only share, giving all your users the same content

Folder redirection is configured through group policies as shown in the following screenshot:

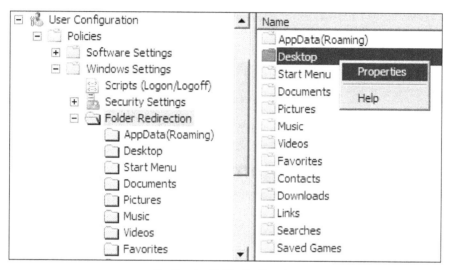

Configuring Folder Redirection

For each folder, you can choose to redirect it to a fixed location (useful if you want to provide the same content to all your users), to a subfolder (named as the username) under a fixed root path to the user's home directory, or to the local user profile location.

You may also apply different redirections based on group membership and define advanced settings for the Documents folder.

In my experience, folder redirection plays a key role in speeding up the logon process. You should enable it at least for the Desktop and My Documents folder if you're using roaming profiles.

Background upload

With Windows 2008 R2, Microsoft added the ability to perform periodic upload of the user's profile registry file (NTUSER.DAT) on the file share. Even if this option wasn't added to address the last write wins problem, it may help to avoid profile corruption and Microsoft recommends enabling it through a GPO as shown in the following screenshot:

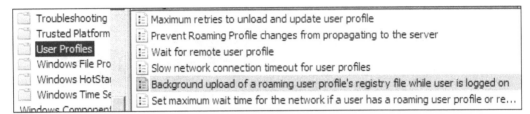

Enabling Background upload

Citrix Profile Management

Citrix developed its own solution for managing profiles, Citrix Profile Management.

You're entitled to use Citrix Profile Management if you have an active Subscription Advantage for the following products:

- XenApp Enterprise and Platinum edition
- XenDesktop Advanced, Enterprise, and Platinum edition

You need to install the software on each computer whose user profiles you want to manage. In a XenApp farm install it on your session-host servers.

Features

Citrix Profile Management was designed specifically to solve some of the problems Windows roaming profiles introduced. Its main features are:

- Support for multiple sessions, without the last write wins problem
- Ability to manage large profiles, without the need to perform a full sync when the user logs on

- Support for v1 (Windows XP/2003) and v2 (Windows Vista/Seven/2008) profiles
- Ability to define inclusion/exclusion lists
- Extended synchronization can include files and folders external to the profile to support legacy applications

Configuring

Citrix Profile Management is configured using Windows Group Policy.

In the Profile Management package, downloadable from the Citrix website, you can find the administrative template (.admx) and its language file (.adml). Copy the ADMX file in C:\Windows\PolicyDefintions and the ADML file in C:\Windows\PolicyDefintions\lang (for example, on English operating systems the lang folder is en-US).

A new **Profile Management** folder in **Citrix** is then available in your GPOs as shown in the following screenshot:

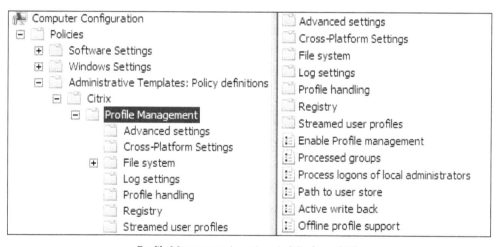

Profile Management's settings in Windows GPOs

Profile Management settings are in the **Computer** section, therefore, link the GPO to the **Organizational Unit (OU)** that contains your session-host servers.

Profiles priority order

If you deployed Citrix Profile Management, it takes precedence over any other profile assignment method. The priority order on a XenApp server is the following:

- Citrix Profile Management
- Remote Desktop Services profile assigned by a GPO
- Remote Desktop Services profile assigned by a user property
- Roaming profile assigned by a GPO
- Roaming profile assigned by a user property

Troubleshooting

Citrix Profile Management includes a logging functionality, you can enable via GPO as shown in the following screenshot:

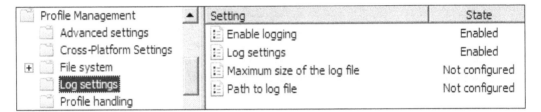

Enabling the logging functionality

With the **Log settings** setting, you can also enable verbose logging for specific events or actions.

Logs are usually saved in `%SystemRoot%\System32\Logfiles\UserProfileManager` but you can change the path with the **Path to log file** property.

Profile Management's logs are also useful to troubleshoot slow logons. Each step is logged with a timestamp so analyzing those logs you can find which steps last for a long time.

GPO and logon script issues

In a Windows environment, it's common to apply settings and customizations via **Group Policy Objects** (**GPOs**) or using logon scripts.

Numerous GPOs and long-running scripts can significantly impact the speed of the logon process. It's sometimes hard to find which GPOs or scripts are causing delays. A suggestion is to move the XenApp server or a test user account in a new Organizational Unit, with no policies applied and blocked inheritance. Comparing the logon time in this scenario with the normal logon time can help you understand how GPOs and scripts affect the logon process.

The following are some of the best practices when working with GPOs and logon scripts:

- Reduce the number of GPOs by merging them when possible. The time Windows takes to apply 10 GPOs is much more than the time to apply a single GPO including all their settings.

- Disable unused GPOs sections. It's common to have GPOs with only computer or user settings. Explicitly disabling the unused sections can speed up the time required to apply the GPOs.

- Use GPOs instead of logon scripts. Windows 2008 introduced **Group Policy Preferences**, which can be used to perform common tasks (map network drives, change registry keys, and so on) previously performed by logon scripts. The following screenshot displays configuring drive maps through GPOs:

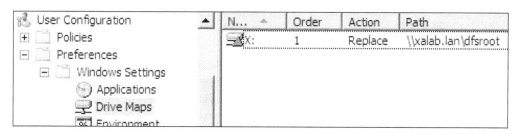

Configuring drive maps through GPO

- Assign logon scripts to users via GPOs rather than the user account property setting.

Session pre-launch, sharing, and lingering

Setting up a session is the most time-consuming task Citrix and Windows have to perform when a user requests an application. In the latest version of XenApp, Citrix added some features to anticipate the session setup (pre-launch) and to improve the sharing of the same session between different applications (lingering).

Session pre-launch

Session pre-launch is a new feature of XenApp 6.5. Instead of waiting for the user to launch an application, you can configure XenApp to set up a session as soon as the user logs on to the farm.

[At the moment, session pre-launch works only if the user logs on using the Receiver, not through the Web Interface.]

This means that when the user requests an application, a session is already loaded and all the steps of the logon process you've learned have already taken place. The application can start without any delay. From my experience, this is a feature much appreciated by users and I use it in the production farms.

Please note that if you enable session pre-launch, a license is consumed at the time the user logs on.

Configuring

A session pre-launch is based on a published application on your farm. A common mistake is thinking that when you configure a pre-launch application, Citrix effectively launches that application when the user logs on. The application is actually used as a template for the session. Citrix uses some of its settings, like users, servers/worker groups, color depth, and so on.

To create a pre-launch session, right-click on the application and choose **Other Tasks | Create pre-launch application** as shown in the following screenshot:

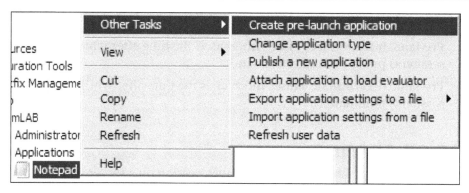

Creating pre-launch application

To avoid confusion, I suggest renaming the configured pre-launch session removing the actual application name, for example, you can name it `Pre-launch WGProd`.

A pre-launched session can be used to run applications that have the same settings of the application you chose when you created the session. For example, it can be used by applications that run on the same servers. If you published different groups of applications, usually assigned to different worker groups, you should create pre-launch sessions choosing one application for each group to be sure that all your users' benefit from this feature.

Life cycle of a session

If you configured a pre-launch session, when the Receiver passes the user credentials to the XenApp server a new session is created. The server that will host the session is chosen in the usual way by the Data Collector.

In Citrix AppCenter, you can identify pre-launched sessions from the value in the **Application State** column as shown in the following screenshot:

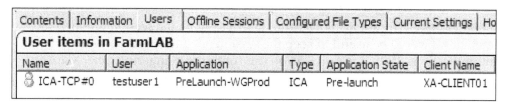

Pre-launched session

Using Citrix policies, you can set the maximum time a pre-launch session is kept:

- **Pre-launch Disconnect Timer Interval**, is the time after which the pre-launch session is put in disconnected state

- **Pre-launch Terminate Timer Interval**, is the time after which the pre-launch session is terminated

Session sharing

Session sharing occurs when a user has an open session on a server and launches an application that is published on the same server. The launch time for the second application is quicker because Citrix doesn't need to set up a new session for it.

Session sharing is enabled by default if you publish your applications in seamless window mode. In this mode, applications appear in their own windows without containing an ICA session window. They seem physically installed on the client.

Session sharing fails if applications are published with different settings (for example, color depth, encryption, and so on). Make sure to publish your applications using the same settings if possible.

Session sharing takes precedence over load balancing; the only exception is if the server reports full load.

 You can force XenApp to override the load check and to also use fully loaded servers for session sharing. Refer to CTX126839 for the requested registry changes. This is, however, not a recommended configuration; a fully loaded server can lead to poor performance.

Session lingering

If a user closes all the applications running in a session, the session is ended too. Sometimes it would be useful to keep the session open to speed up the start of new applications. With XenApp 6.5 you can configure a lingering time. XenApp waits before closing a session even if all the running applications are closed.

Configuring

With Citrix user policies, you can configure two timers for session lingering:

- **Linger Disconnect Timer Interval**, is the time after which a session without applications is put in disconnected state

- **LingerTerminate Timer Interval**, is the time after which a session without applications is terminated

 If you're running an older version of XenApp, you can keep a session open even if users close all the running applications with the **KeepMeLoggedIn** tool; refer to CTX128579.

Summary

The optimization of the logon process can greatly improve the user experience. With EdgeSight and Windows Performance Toolkit you can perform a deep analysis and detect any causes of delay. If you can't use those tools, you are still able to implement some guidelines and best practices that will surely make users' logon faster.

Setting up a session is a time-consuming task. With XenApp 6.5, Citrix implemented some new features to improve session management. With session pre-launch and session lingering you can maximize the reuse of existing sessions when users request an application, speeding up its launch time.

4
Improving End User Experience

When I started working with Citrix MetaFrame, the ancestor of XenApp, it was mainly used to publish business applications, like ERP or mainframe's terminal emulators, so there was no need for multimedia features.

In the last few years, I needed to publish more and more multimedia applications to my users. With the adoption of thin clients, all the applications including CAD applications, media players, and internet browsers, had to run on XenApp servers. In addition, some business applications now use graphical effects (transitions, transparencies, and so on) that benefit from hardware acceleration.

In this chapter you'll learn:

- How to optimize the Windows GUI for applications published with XenApp
- Which features XenApp offers for multimedia redirection
- What is Citrix HDX and how to use its features to deliver a high-definition experience

Optimizing Windows GUI

Changing the default Windows behavior may improve the user experience when the entire desktop or a single application is delivered by XenApp.

Windows settings

Some optimizations are configured on Windows side.

Menu show delay

Windows normally delays menus before they are displayed. You can reduce the delay by changing the following registry key:

```
HKCU\Control Panel\Desktop\MenuShowDelay
```

The default value on Windows 2008 is 400. You can set it from 0 to 4000 milliseconds.

Internet Explorer offscreen composition

If websites contain animated content, sometimes the content may flicker if viewed with Internet Explorer running over a Terminal Services session.

You can force IE to render the content offscreen by creating the following registry key:

```
HKCU\Software\Microsoft\Internet Explorer\Main\Force Offscreen
Composition=00000001 (dword)
```

 With IE9, Microsoft removed the Force Offscreen Composition setting, so adding the preceding key will affect only IE8 or earlier versions.

Screensaver

A screensaver running in a XenApp session consumes CPU cycles and is normally useless. In case you need to lock the user's workstation, a local screensaver would be a better option. If your policies require a screensaver on the server, use a blank one.

The best way to disable the screensaver is through a Windows GPO applied to your users. The following screenshot displays disabling screensaver with GPO:

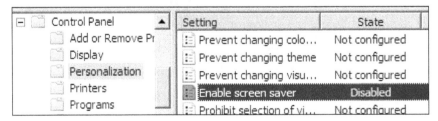

Disabling screensaver with GPO

Auto end tasks

When a user logs off, sometimes an application becomes unresponsive. Windows presents a dialog with the options of **Wait** or **End task**. You can suppress the dialog and automatically end the unresponsive task with the following registry value:

```
HKCU\Control Panel\Desktop\AutoEndTasks=1 (REG_SZ)
```

You can set the maximum wait time before auto ending the task with the following value:

```
HKCU\Control Panel\Desktop\WaittoKillAppTimeout=seconds (REG_SZ)
```

Citrix settings

Other optimizations are configured through the Citrix policies.

Desktop UI – user policy

If you're publishing applications with seamless window mode, the desktop is hidden from the users. You can therefore disable wallpapers and animations without affecting the user experience.

Displaying window content while dragging is a feature that consumes memory and network bandwidth. I usually disable it too. The following screenshot displays disabling **Desktop UI** features:

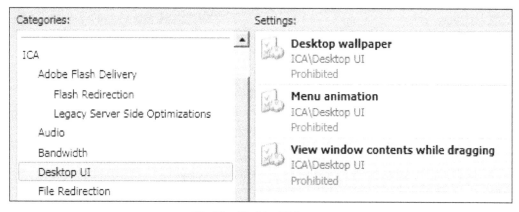

Disabling Desktop UI features

Graphics – computer policy

By default, XenApp limits the display memory available for a single session to 32768 kilobytes. If this limit is, reached, XenApp degrades the color depth of the session. Furthermore, XenApp queues images before sending them to the client. If a queued image is replaced by another one, XenApp discards the first one and doesn't send it to the client. This feature is known as **image tossing**.

The previous settings are included in the **Graphics** category. I found increasing the memory limit useful sometimes, especially when working with CAD applications. If users complain about choppy videos, try disabling the queuing and tossing feature.

Dynamic Windows Preview is a feature Microsoft added in the latest versions of Windows. By default if you publish applications with seamless window mode, the client OS can display dynamic previews for those applications. You can disable this feature to save bandwidth. The following screenshot displays the changing **Graphics** settings:

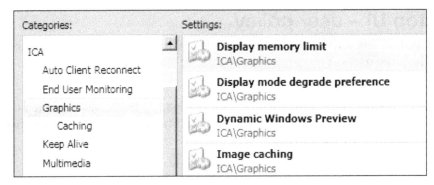

Changing Graphics settings

Visual Display – computer policy

The **Visual Display** category, as shown in the following screenshot, contains settings that may improve the responsiveness of the application at the expense of display quality. So before applying them be sure to perform a test with your users.

With the **Max Frames Per Second** setting, you can increase/decrease the default number of frames per second (24). Sometimes you may need to increase it (up to 30 fps) for applications like 3D CAD. On the other hand you could decrease it to save bandwidth, especially when publishing applications don't require frequent screen updates (for example, terminal emulators). This setting may greatly affect resources and bandwidth usage, so be careful and test any changes.

Moving Images and **Still Images** settings allow you to apply different compression levels on screen images. You could use these settings if you need to save bandwidth:

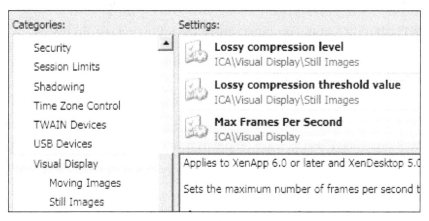

Changing Visual Display settings

Citrix HDX

HDX stands for **High Definition eXperience.** It's more than a technology; it's a brand that encapsulates several different features, some of which were already previously available with different names.

Citrix created the HDX brand to group together all the elements that deliver high-definition experience to XenApp/XenDesktop users. HDX is designed to take advantage, when possible, of the processing power of end user devices.

HDX MediaStream

HDX MediaStream is a set of features to optimize the delivery of video/audio content.

It offloads, when possible, the rendering of media content to the user device, reducing server's CPU load and bandwidth usage. Because the media content is processed on the user's device, the playback is not affected by latency.

Flash redirection

Adobe Flash is a technology adopted in many websites, including YouTube and other video-hosting services. It's also used in some web applications, for example, the management console of VMware View.

You can configure HDX MediaStream to move the processing of Flash content from the published Internet Explorer to the end user device. At the moment, this feature supports only Internet Explorer (versions 7, 8, and 9), not Firefox or Chrome.

To enable Flash redirection, you must satisfy the following requirements:

- On the user device, install Receiver for Linux 12.0 or Receiver for Windows 3.0 or higher

- On the user device, install Flash player for other browsers

- On the session-host servers, install Flash player for Internet Explorer

- Make sure the Flash version on the user device is equal to or higher than the version on the server

Adobe Flash Player

Adobe published two versions of its Flash Player: one for Internet Explorer (sometimes known as ActiveX player) and the other for browsers supporting **NPAPI (Netscape Plugin Application Programming Interface)** like Firefox and Chrome. You need both versions, the first for session-host servers and the second for user devices.

A category of settings is available in Citrix user policies to enable and configure the **Flash Redirection** feature as shown in the following screenshot:

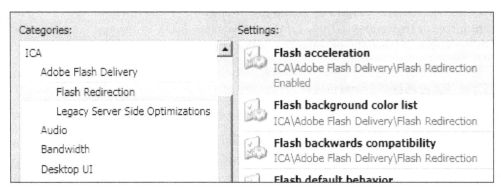

Configuring Flash redirection with Citrix policies

On the client side, you can tune this feature using Windows Group Policy Objects.

An administrative template (.ADM) file is available in the following path:

```
%Program Files%\Citrix\ICA Client\Configuration\language
```

or, if you are on a 64-bit system:

```
%Program Files (x86)%\Citrix\ICA Client\Configuration\language
```

 With XenApp 6.5, Citrix introduced a second generation Flash redirection, adding **intelligent failback mode**, that detects situations in which the feature is unnecessary, and supporting **WAN** connections.

Windows Media redirection

XenApp is able to send multimedia files to the client in the original, compressed format and use the client's resources to decompress and render them. This feature is similar to the Flash redirection introduced before.

 If the user device runs Linux, you must install GStreamer if your distribution doesn't already include it.

You can enable this feature and tune the buffer size using Citrix computer policies. The following screenshot displays configuring **Windows Media Redirection** with Citrix policies:

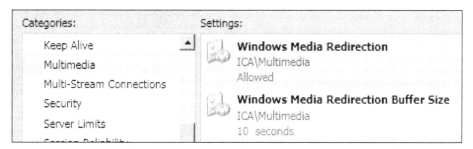

Configuring Windows Media Redirection with Citrix policies

HDX RealTime

HDX RealTime was designed to optimize interaction between audio peripherals connected to the user device and applications running on virtual desktops or hosted in the datacenter.

HDX RealTime supports two different approaches:

- Generic HDX RealTime
- Optimized HDX RealTime

Generic HDX RealTime

The first approach allows the use of any softphone or unified communication application without the need to modify it.

Before XenApp 6.5, only the default audio device of the endpoint was available for a published application, redirected with the standard name Citrix HDX Audio. With version 6.5, Citrix added a true Plug and Play for audio devices. When you connect a new device to the endpoint, it's made available to the published applications with its own name as shown in the following screenshot:

The new Plug and Play functionality in XenApp 6.5

Citrix uses an Optimized-for-Speech codec to compress the audio streams and send them over the ICA protocol, which supports multiple data streams. By default audio traffic is assigned the highest priority, ensuring low latency.

If a video stream is also present, it's rendered by the application on the server and analyzed by Adaptive Display, which dynamically adjusts the compression level and frame rate to deliver the best possible quality for the available bandwidth.

 Make sure to have installed the Hotfix Rollup Pack 1 for XenApp 6.5 to enable Adaptive Display. At the moment this feature is not configurable in XenApp using Citrix policies, but via Windows GPOs.

Optimized HDX RealTime

If you consider a generic softphone or unified communication client, you can logically split it into three layers: the user interface, the business logic, and the media engine. The media engine is the layer that handles signaling, encoding, and decoding of audio and video traffic. The idea behind this approach is to move the media engine layer to the user device. The Citrix server no longer needs to handle audio and video streams, reducing bandwidth consumption and server load.

The business logic and media engine layers still need a way to communicate. The interprocess communication has to occur over the network on a virtual channel as shown in the following diagram:

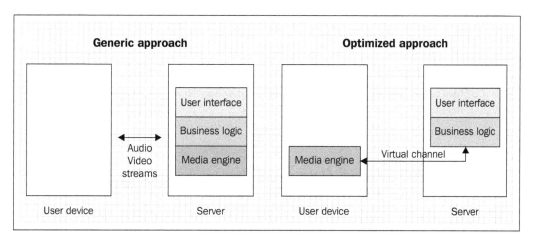

Generic approach versus Optimized approach

Implementing this architecture requires a change in the application. Both Avaya and Cisco now offer a VDI-optimized version of their VoIP clients.

Sometimes, the vendor offers a way a third party could use to modify how calls are initiated and managed. For example, Citrix used Microsoft APIs to deploy an optimization pack for Lync (formerly known as Office Communicator).

The optimization pack consists of two components:

- Citrix HDX RealTime Media Engine, that runs on the user device
- Citrix HDX RealTime Connector, that runs on the server and connects the Lync client to the media engine

Often system administrators consider VDI solutions like XenApp/XenDesktop or VMWare View not yet ready for real-time applications like VoIP clients. I used the Lync optimization pack to publish about one hundred clients. The audio and video quality is similar to local clients and it didn't require many server resources.

HDX RichGraphics

With the HDX RichGraphics feature, XenApp can optimize the performance of 2D and 3D applications offloading the rendering process to the server's GPU.

By default, XenApp moves the rendering of DirectX and Direct3D applications to the server's GPU if available. No additional configuration is needed. You can also enable the offloading of **Windows Presentation Foundation (WPF)** applications adding the following registry value:

```
EnableWPFHook = 1 (REG_DWORD)
```

in the key:

```
HKLM\Software\Wow6432Node\Citrix\CtxHook\AppInit_Dlls\Multiple
Monitor Hook
```

OpenGL

You can offload the rendering of OpenGL applications by installing an optional XenApp component, OpenGL GPU Sharing Feature Add-on, available on Citrix's website.

GPU offloading in a virtual environment

To enable GPU offloading, your XenApp servers need a direct connection to the GPU. If you run the servers in a virtual environment, you must configure the GPU in pass-through mode. This mode, which is available in Citrix XenServer and VMWare vSphere (sometimes referred as VMDirectPath I/O), directly connects the graphic card to a virtual machine.

HDX Monitor

HDX Monitor is a free tool, available on Citrix's website (`http://hdx.citrix.com/hdx-monitor`). You can use it to get technical details about HDX and to troubleshoot any problems. Install the tool on any machine in your domain and enter one of your XenApp servers as the target.

HDX Monitor displays the status of the different HDX components (Media and Flash redirection, Audio subsystem, and so on), and for each of them you can obtain status details and bandwidth usage.

This is a very useful tool to verify which HDX features are actually running. HDX Monitor also gives you suggestions, warnings and errors about the analyzed system as shown in the following screenshot:

 Adaptive (or Progressive) display schemes are recommended for low bandwidth environments.
more details...

 Turn on extra color compression to improve bandwidth utilization.
more details...

 Adaptive display is disabled by policy.

 Higher compression results in lower image quality. Use higher compression only for low bandwidth connections. Use lower compression for LAN environments.

HDX Monitor's suggestions and warnings

Summary

A common myth is that desktop and application virtualization technologies are only good for "office" applications.

With some optimizations and tuning and leveraging technologies provided by Citrix HDX, you can offer a high definition user experience to your XenApp users. With HDX Monitor, you can check if all the features are running and inspect any problems.

5
Optimizing for WAN Links

If you're administering a XenApp farm for a while, someone has probably already asked you to give access to published applications for users who are not connected to your local LAN. The external access could be for teleworkers, for branch offices, or for outsourcers that even work in a different continent.

The **Independent Computing Architecture (ICA)** protocol is known for its excellent performance over slow links and its low bandwidth usage. In this chapter you'll learn:

- The differences between LAN and WAN links
- The specific optimizations available in XenApp for WAN links
- How to test your farm's behavior over WAN links before going to production

Characteristics of a WAN link

The most general definition of a **Wide Area Network (WAN)** is a network that covers a broad area, using public or private network transports. In this chapter, we're going to analyze the scenario of a remote user who needs to access an application published by a XenApp farm located in your datacenter.

The connection between the user and your infrastructure may be on a private link (usually a leased line) or on a public network (usually the Internet). The most important parameters of a link are:

- The available bandwidth
- The latency
- The reliability

A common belief is that **bandwidth** is the main problem in remote connections; this is usually false. A fast access to the Internet is now available in most countries and also mobile operators can offer high-speed connections (HDSPA, LTE, and so on). Dedicated links can be leased with guaranteed bandwidth and, with technologies such as MPLS, carriers now offer geographic links with high speed.

The **latency**, on the contrary, depends on the distance between the two endpoints of a link and the transmission medium; it's usually a fixed value.

For example, let's consider a satellite link. Geosynchronous satellites orbit at about 42 km from the Earth; radio signals take about 250 ms to reach them, so this type of link introduces a fixed delay of 500 ms, as shown in the following diagram:

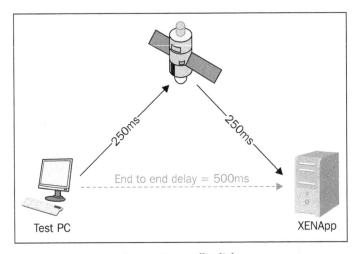

Latency in a satellite link

A high value of latency is very problematic, especially with graphical applications. Later in this chapter you'll learn some advanced features of XenApp that you can use to minimize the impact of the latency on the user experience.

Emulating links with WANem

If you're planning to publish applications on geographic links, it's very important to test how those applications perform and you'll learn later in this chapter, how the optimizations work for improving the user experience.

Plan a complete **UAT (User Acceptance Test)** phase before going to production, if possible with real users. In this paragraph you'll learn how to use an opensource tool, WANem, to emulate a WAN link.

I usually prepare some test scenarios, and ask users to give a score from 1 (bad) to 5 (good) for the user experience. Here's an example of the feedbacks I got from a test session, varying bandwidth (columns) and latency (rows) and without any optimizations:

Time	100 Kb/s	200 Kb/s	300 Kb/s	500 Kb/s
10 ms	2	3	4	5
50 ms	2	2	3	4
150 ms	1	1	1	2

Installing

WANem is distributed as a bootable CD, based on Linux Knoppix. The operating system runs live from the CD, that is, you don't need to install it on the machine's hard disk.

WANem does not require many resources; any i386 PC or server with at least 1 GB RAM will be ok. The administrative interface is web based so you can configure WANem from any device with a web browser.

The ISO image is downloadable from the official website: `http://wanem.sourceforge.net`.

During the boot process, you'll be asked for network parameters; WANem supports both DHCP and manual configuration, as shown in the following screenshot:

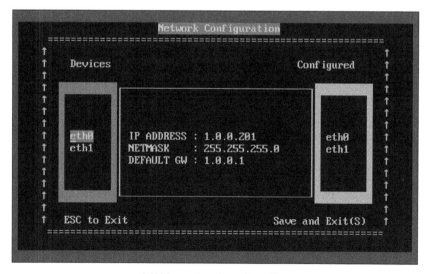

WANem network configuration

At the end of the boot process, you're presented with a command prompt: WANem is ready and you can connect to its web interface, `http://WANemIP/WANem`.

Configuring

In order to be able to emulate a WAN link, you have to force the packets between a test client and your XenApp server to flow via WANem. The simplest and suggested way is to place all the three devices on the same network and to configure **static routes** on the PC and the server, as shown in the following diagram:

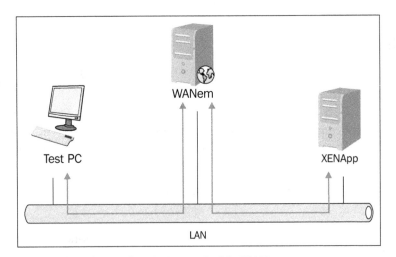

Packet routing required for WANem

Let's assume the following IP addresses:

- Test PC (XA-CLIENT01): 1.0.0.200
- XenApp Server (XA-APP01): 1.0.0.20
- WANem virtual appliance (XA-WANEM): 1.0.0.201

On the client, you have to configure a static route to send the packets destinated with destination to the server through the WANem appliance:

`C:\>route add 1.0.0.20 mask 255.255.255.255 1.0.0.201`

On the other hand, on the server you have to configure a static route for the returning traffic (from the server to the client):

`C:\>route add 1.0.0.200 mask 255.255.255.255 1.0.0.201`

To verify that the routing is working, start an infinite PING command from the client to the server:

```
C:\>ping -t 1.0.0.20
```

You should see the replies coming from the server in a few milliseconds.

Now connect to the WANem web interface, choose **Basic Mode**, insert a delay time of 100 ms and click on **Apply settings**, as shown in the following screenshot:

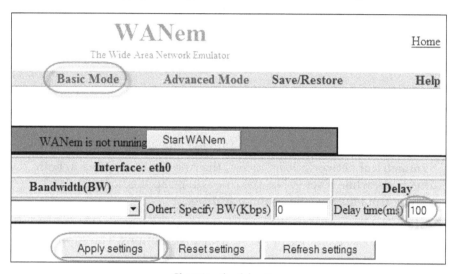

Changing the delay time

If the configuration is ok, you should now see the replies to the PING command coming with about 200 ms of delay, as shown in the following screenshot:

```
Reply from 1.0.0.20: bytes=32 time<1ms TTL=127
Reply from 1.0.0.20: bytes=32 time<1ms TTL=127
Reply from 1.0.0.20: bytes=32 time<1ms TTL=127
Reply from 1.0.0.20: bytes=32 time<1ms TTL=127
Reply from 1.0.0.20: bytes=32 time<1ms TTL=127
Reply from 1.0.0.20: bytes=32 time<1ms TTL=127
Reply from 1.0.0.20: bytes=32 time=204ms TTL=127
Reply from 1.0.0.20: bytes=32 time=203ms TTL=127
Reply from 1.0.0.20: bytes=32 time=205ms TTL=127
```

Differences in reply time with WANem enabled

Using

Through WANem web interface, you can change the settings of the emulated link.

In Basic Mode, you can set the bandwidth (choosing from standard values or entering custom ones) and delay (latency). Only one rule is possible for each network interface.

The emulated link is symmetrical; that's why in the previous example if you set a delay of 100 ms, the **RTT (Round Trip Time)** measured by the PING command is 200 ms.

In **Advanced Mode**, you can add different rules, based on source and destination addresses.

For each rule, you can define specific network characteristics:

- **Packet limit**: The maximum number of packets WANem can keep in the forwarding queue. If the queue is full, the new packets are discarded.

- **Symmetrical network**: If set to Yes, the rule will be applied in both directions; while if set to No, the rule will be applied only for packets coming from the specified source address.

- **Delay**: The latency of the link. You can specify a static value, add a random jitter, or choose from one of the statistic distributions. The supported delay resolution is 10 ms, so use multiples of that value.

- **Loss**: The percentage of packets that will be randomly dropped. With the optional correlation value, you can emulate packet burst losses.

- **Duplication**: The percentage of packets that will be randomly duplicated. With the optional correlation value, you can emulate packet burst duplications.

- **Corruption**: The percentage of packets that will be randomly corrupted. WANem introduces a single bit error at a random offset in the packet.

- **Reordering**: The percentage of packets that will be forwarded out of sequence.

- **Bandwidth**: The available bandwidth. For a good accuracy, don't go lower than 120 Kb/s.

- **Disconnection**: This is used to simulate an unreliable network. You can choose how WANem emulates disconnections (TCP resets, ICMP messages, and so on) and, for random disconnection, the **MTTF (Mean Time To Failure)** and **MTTR (Mean Time To Recovery)** values.

WANalyzer

WANem can be used also to analyze a WAN link. WANalyzer is able to measure the following network characteristics of the connection to a target host:

- Latency
- Loss of packets
- Jitter
- Available bandwidth

The following screenshot displays these characteristics:

RESULTS	
Remote host IP	1.0.0.20
Time of measurement	13:54:28
Latency	89.96 ms
Loss of packet	0 %
Jitter	89.9602
Available Band Width	1.29752 Mbps

WANalyzer result

Optimizing the ICA protocol

The ICA protocol is a proprietary protocol designed by Citrix and is used for client/server communication in XenApp and XenDesktop. It runs over TCP port 1494 but it may be encapsulated in **CGP** (**Common Gateway Protocol**) over TCP port 2598. You'll learn the importance of CGP later in this chapter.

 Citrix offers a service-centric WAN optimization solution, with physical and virtual appliances, named **NetScaler Branch Repeater**.

ICA Virtual Channels

The ICA protocol comprises virtual channels, as shown in the following diagram. A virtual channel consists of a driver, running on the client side, which communicates with a server-side application. It transports data for redirected peripherals (keyboard, printer, and so on) or for Citrix functionalities (clipboard, licensing, and so on). A couple of channels are also available for **Original Equipment Manufacturers (OEMs)**.

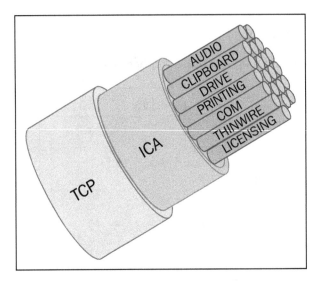

Virtual Channels in ICA protocol

Virtual Channel Priorities

The ICA protocol implements an internal **Quality of Service (QoS)**, assigning different priorities to different virtual channel groups.

The protocol defines the following four priorities:

- 0 = very high
- 1 = high
- 2 = medium
- 3 = low

The following table displays the virtual channels and their default priority:

Name	Description	Priority
CTXCAM	Client audio mapping	0
CTXTW	ThinWire – Remote Windows screen update data	1
CTXTWI	ThinWire – Seamless Windows screen update data	1
CTXLIC	License management	1
CTXVFM	Video Server	1
CTXPN	Program Neighbourhood	1
CTXSBR	No longer used, was Browser Acceleration	1
CTXSCRD	Smartcard redirection	1
CTXCTL	Citrix Control	1
CTXEUEM	End User Experience Monitoring	1
CTXMM	Windows Multimedia redirection	2
CTXFLSH	Flash redirection	2
CTXGUSB	USB redirection	2
CTXCLIP	Clipboard redirection	2
CTXCDM	Client Drive mapping	2
CTXCCM	Client COM port mapping	3
CTXCM	Client management (autoupdate)	3
CTXLPT1-2	Printer mapping for non-spooling clients (parallel)	3
CTXCOM1-2	Printer mapping for non-spooling clients (serial)	3
CTXCPM	Printer mapping for spooling clients	3
OEMOEM	Used by OEMs	3
OEMOEM2		

You can change the priority assigned to a virtual channel with the **VirtualChannels** value in the registry key located at `HKLM\System\CurrentControlSet\Control\` `Terminal Server\Wds\icawd\MultiStreamIca\`

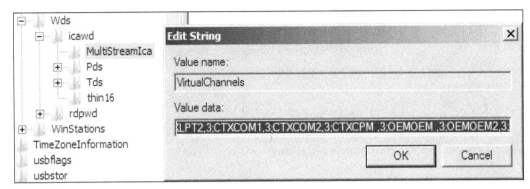

Changing virtual channels' priority

ICA MultiStream

With the use of virtual channel's priority, you can implement a QoS within the single ICA connection. Network devices have no visibility of the different virtual channels, so you can't give priority to a specific channel with network-based QoS. For example, if you're experiencing poor audio quality due to network congestion caused by both ICA and non-ICA traffic, network administrators can only prioritize the entire ICA session.

With XenApp 6.5, Citrix added a new feature, ICA MultiStream. ICA MultiStream uses different TCP connections for the classes of service; each TCP connection binds to a different TCP port on the server and network administrators can apply different QoS classes to the different connections.

The following diagram displays the differences between normal mode and MultiStream:

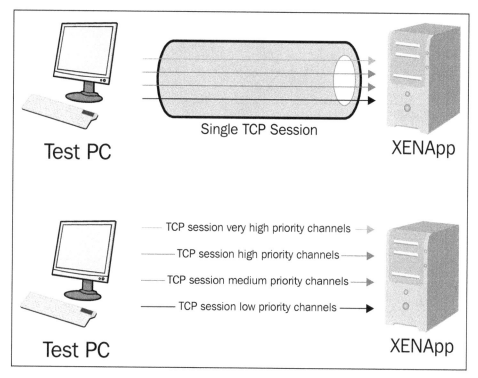

Differences between "normal" mode and MultiStream

 ICA MultiStream requires Session Reliability enabled. Session Reliability buffers the traffic, tunneling it with CGP, to avoid disconnections due to network blips.

Enabling ICA MultiStream

ICA MultiStream is controlled by Citrix policies.

First, you need to enable it at server level, with a computer policy:

```
ICA\Multi-Stream Connections\Multi-Stream = Enabled
```

Then, with the **Multi-Port Policy**, you can define up to four different TCP ports and assign them to the different priorities, as shown in the following screenshot:

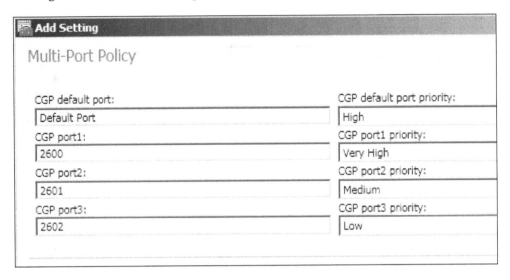

 Make sure the chosen ports are not already used by other services on your XenApp servers. With the `netstat -na` command you can list the ports in LISTENING state.

Finally, enable the Multi-Stream feature also in user policies; by default, indeed, it's disabled for all users.

Traffic shaping

In some scenarios, it is very important to limit the maximum bandwidth used by different sessions. Even if you're using a high-speed link, shaping some streams is a good practice. Consider, for example, a user working with a scanner; when the scanner sends the image to the application running on the XenApp server, it can easily saturate the available bandwidth.

XenApp offers a category of user policies to limit the bandwidth used by the different supported redirections, as shown in the following screenshot:

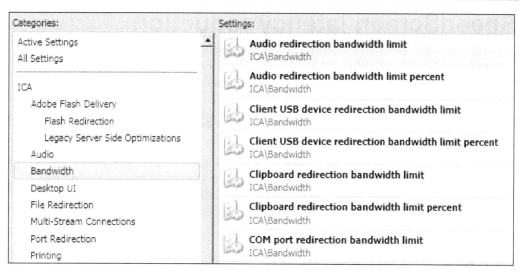

Limit the bandwidth used by XenApp

You can limit the overall session bandwidth and/or the bandwidth used for:

- Audio redirection
- Client USB device redirection
- Clipboard redirection
- COM port redirection
- File redirection
- HDX MediaStream redirection
- LPT port redirection
- Printer redirection
- TWAIN device redirection

You can define a fixed limit value (in Kb per second) and a percentage of the total session bandwidth. If you configure both the two settings, the most restrictive one is applied.

SpeedScreen latency reduction

XenApp offers two features to enhance user experience on high latency connections: Mouse Click Feedback and Local Text Echo. These two features are often referred to with the collective term of SpeedScreen Latency Reduction.

 SpeedScreen was the name Citrix used before introducing the HDX brand.

Both the features are configured a specific tool, SpeedScreen Latency Reduction Manager. You can find it by navigating to **Administrative Tools | Citrix | Administration Tools**. You need at least local administrative rights to run the tool.

Mouse Click Feedback

On a slow network, users don't receive an immediate feedback for mouse clicks, so they often click multiple times.

If you enable Mouse Click Feedback, Citrix Receiver, running on the user's machine, immediately changes the mouse pointer from idle to busy after the user clicks, to show that the command is being processed and to avoid multiple clicks by the user.

This feature is enabled by default; you can disable it at the server level.

From the SpeedScreen Latency Reduction Manager, navigate to **Application | Server Properties...** In the same dialog, you can set the low and high thresholds for activating SpeedScreen functionalities.

Local Text Echo

If the network latency is high, users could experience significant delays between when they type a character on the keyboard and when it is displayed on the screen. The keystrokes indeed are sent to the application running on the server; this renders the fonts and sends back the updated screen to the client.

The Local Text Echo feature, disabled by default, temporarily renders the text using local fonts and immediately displays it on the screen, without waiting for the screen redraw from the server.

You can enable this feature at the server level (check the corresponding option in the server properties dialog) or for a specific application. You can also configure it only for specific input fields (for example, the login dialog of your application).

Adding applications

If you want to enable Local Text Echo only for some applications or you need to change the default settings because a published application doesn't work with Local Text Echo, first you have to add those applications in the SpeedScreen Latency Reduction Manager.

Start the application, then right-click on the server and choose **Add New Application...**

Drag the pointer on the running application; the wizard automatically identifies its path, as shown in the following screenshot:

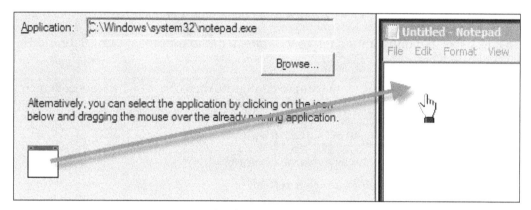

Identifying the application

Choose if Local Text Echo should be enabled for the application and if the previous setting is for all the installations of the application (that is, Local Text Echo doesn't consider the specific path but only the application name) or only for the one selected.

> If you need to propagate the same configuration to other servers, you can copy the content of the C:\Program Files (x86)\Citrix\ss3config folder where all the settings are saved. Make sure you chose **Apply settings to all installations of the selected application** if paths to the published application differ on your servers.

Configuring applications

To configure specific settings for an added application, right-click on it, and choose **Application Properties...**.

You can completely disable Local Text Echo or limit its functionalities:

- **Display text in place** displays text only in the text fields
- **Display text in a floating bubble**, doesn't render text locally but displays "bubbles" until the server finishes processing

You can also disable both Local Text Echo and Mouse Click Feedback for input files (thread them in native mode).

Configuring input fields

You can adjust Local Text Echo settings for specific input fields of your application.

To add a specific configuration for an input field, in the **Input Field Configuration** tab, click on **New**.

Drag the pointer to the field you want to configure, then choose which SpeedScreen functionality level (medium, low, or off) to apply.

For each added field, you can set different options:

- **Limit local text echo** as explained before
- **Reduce font size** for a quicker refresh
- **Use system default colors** for accelerating the rendering
- **Input field is a password** for displaying asterisks or spaces instead of the typed characters

Summary

A common request from users is to access their applications outside the company, using different types of connections. The ICA protocol used by XenApp is designed to work also with low-speed, high-latency connections; system administrators can also use some advanced features to improve the user experience.

WANem is a precious tool to simulate how applications behave with different connections.

Index

Thank you for buying
Citrix XenApp Performance Essentials

About Packt Publishing

Packt, pronounced 'packed', published its first book "Mastering phpMyAdmin for Effective MySQL Management" in April 2004 and subsequently continued to specialize in publishing highly focused books on specific technologies and solutions.

Our books and publications share the experiences of your fellow IT professionals in adapting and customizing today's systems, applications, and frameworks. Our solution based books give you the knowledge and power to customize the software and technologies you're using to get the job done. Packt books are more specific and less general than the IT books you have seen in the past. Our unique business model allows us to bring you more focused information, giving you more of what you need to know, and less of what you don't.

Packt is a modern, yet unique publishing company, which focuses on producing quality, cutting-edge books for communities of developers, administrators, and newbies alike. For more information, please visit our website: www.packtpub.com.

About Packt Enterprise

In 2010, Packt launched two new brands, Packt Enterprise and Packt Open Source, in order to continue its focus on specialization. This book is part of the Packt Enterprise brand, home to books published on enterprise software – software created by major vendors, including (but not limited to) IBM, Microsoft and Oracle, often for use in other corporations. Its titles will offer information relevant to a range of users of this software, including administrators, developers, architects, and end users.

Writing for Packt

We welcome all inquiries from people who are interested in authoring. Book proposals should be sent to author@packtpub.com. If your book idea is still at an early stage and you would like to discuss it first before writing a formal book proposal, contact us; one of our commissioning editors will get in touch with you.

We're not just looking for published authors; if you have strong technical skills but no writing experience, our experienced editors can help you develop a writing career, or simply get some additional reward for your expertise.

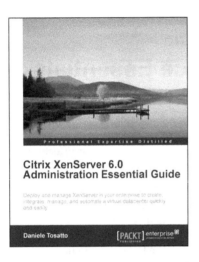

Citrix XenServer 6.0
Administration Essential Guide

Deploy and manage XenServer in your enterprise to create,
integrate, manage, and automate a virtual datacenter quickly
and easily

Daniele Tosatto   [PACKT] enterprise 88

Citrix XenServer 6.0
Administration Essential Guide

ISBN: 978-1-849686-16-7   Paperback: 364 pages

Deploy and manage XenServer in your enterprise
to create, integrate, manage, and automate a virtual
datacenter quickly and easily

1. This book and eBook will take you through
    deploying XenServer in your enterprise, and
    teach you how to create and maintain your
    datacenter

2. Manage XenServer and virtual machines using
    Citrix management tools and the command line

3. Organize secure access to your infrastructure
    using role-based access control

Getting Started with
Citrix XenApp 6.5

Design and implement Citrix farms based on XenApp 6.5

Guillermo Musumeci   [PACKT] enterprise 88

Getting Started with Citrix
XenApp 6.5

ISBN: 978-1-849686-66-2   Paperback: 478 pages

Design and implement Citrix farms based on
XenApp 6.5

1. Use Citrix management tools to publish
    applications and resources on client devices
    with this book and eBook

2. Deploy and optimize XenApp 6.5 on Citrix
    XenServer, VMware ESX, and Microsoft
    Hyper-V virtual machines and physical
    servers

3. Clear, easy-to-follow steps and screenshots
    to carry out each task

Please check **www.PacktPub.com** for information on our titles

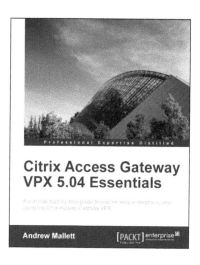

Citrix Access Gateway VPX 5.04 Essentials

ISBN: 978-1-849688-22-2   Paperback: 234 pages

A practical step-by-step guide to provide secure remote access using the Citrix Access Gateway VPX

1. A complete administration companion guiding you through the complexity of providing secure remote access using the Citrix Access Gateway 5 virtual appliance

2. Establish secure access using ICA-Proxy to your Citrix XenApp and XenDesktop hosted environments

3. Use SmartAccess technology to evaluate end users' devices before they connect to your protected network

Implementing Citrix XenServer Quickstarter

ISBN: 978-1-849689-82-3   Paperback: 134 pages

A practical guide to getting started with the Citrix XenServer Virtualization technology with easy-to-follow instructions

1. A simple and quick start guide for any system admin who wants to step into the latest and hottest virtualization technology

2. Learn how to convert physical machines to virtual ones using XenConvert

3. Get to grips with the advanced features of Citrix XenServer

Please check **www.PacktPub.com** for information on our titles

www.ingramcontent.com/pod-product-compliance
Lightning Source LLC
Chambersburg PA
CBHW082122070326
40690CB00049B/4110